HEALING FOR THE MIND

William J. Finnigan, D. Min.

REVIVAL LITERATURE
PO BOX 505
SKYLAND, NC 28776
800-252-8896
www.revivallit.org

Second Edition 1986

Printed in the United S

Dedication

This book is affectionately dedicated to my beloved wife, Christina, who tenderly and faithfully ministered to me during the trying experiences that inspired this writing.

A special word of thanks is due Mrs. Jan Gandee and Mrs. William Sikora, Jr., who ministered so willingly and sacrificially at the typewriter. I am also grateful to Mrs. David Wilson who did the illustrating along with Rev. Bob Doom for his suggestions and invaluable assistance. Rev. and Mrs. Paul Reno were also used of God to prayerfully encourage and assist in this publication. To God be the glory!

Foreword

It gives me great pleasure to recommend Dr. Bill Finnigan's new book, *Healing for the Mind.* It is biblical, academic and very practical having been tested and proven through many years of pastoral counseling.

In all my years of college and seminary training, very little was ever said in the classroom about the spiritual warfare and our victory over Satan and his forces through the shed blood of Christ. It is appalling how few pastors and Christian leaders know that the church of the living God is in a spiritual warfare. At best, they know it intellectually and not in reality. I am convinced Satan wants to keep Christians ignorant of his devices.

After hearing Dr. Finnigan deliver a series of messages on this subject, the late Dr. Avery Rogers of Victoria, Texas, expressed to me that he felt it was one of the most needed messages of our day. I agree. Our churches have been literally paralyzed by the spirit of fear. As Christians, we are either in the conflict or we are a casualty.

May God be pleased to give this book wide circulation. I trust it will become required reading in Bible institutes, Christian colleges and seminaries. "For God hath not given us the spirit of fear; but of power, and of love, and of a sound mind" (II Timothy 1:7).

— David Dickerson, D. Min.
Pastor, Mt. Pisgah Baptist Church, Fairburn, Georgia
and President, Georgia Baptist College

Introduction

The fight is on! Warfare rages in the souls of men who have lost their moorings. This is a day when our bodies are being stuffed and tantalized, while at the same time our minds are cracking. It's the day of "legal" drug addiction, with multitudes dependent upon tranquilizers to maintain a semblance of mental balance. The reality of life and death seems increasingly more difficult to face.

Unfortunately, the effects of this tragic situation have not bypassed the Christian church. Rather, our so-called Bible-believing churches are plagued with professing Christians who display anything but true, Spirit-filled victory over the everyday situations of life. Indeed, believers have failed to appropriate the fullness of Christ through His Word, and have become "unbelieving believers"! The same satanic strategies which overpower the ungodly world have broken through into the church. Depression, divorce, nervous breakdowns, defeat and discouragement, etc., are now prevalent *within* the church as well as without.

What has happened to us? Where are the saints of God who demonstrate that "greater is He that is within us than he that is in the world"? Why are so many saints victims rather than victors; overcome, rather than overcomers? In the context of conflict, the Apostle Paul said that the believer is "more than conqueror" (Romans 8:37). Are these just "words" or is this God's truth? Must the saint of God live in defeat, or can he demonstrate the overcoming grace of God in the midst of a crooked and perverted nation?

It is to these questions that this book speaks. Does the salvation of Jesus Christ not include our minds? While the world seemingly has gone "insane," is there not healing for the mind of the believer? The time has come to speak directly to this issue from a biblical perspective. The need is critical in our day. The world, the flesh and the devil are warring against our minds. Therefore, it behooves us to re-evaluate the implications of biblical salvation as it affects the believer's mental attitude.

This book is not the result of mere academic exercise. It is born in the writer's life after years of spiritual and mental battle. It comes forth to testify biblically that Christ is indeed our "Helmet of Salvation"! Here is a word intended to speak to those who need healing for their minds.

Acknowledgements

For permission to reprint copyrighted material, grateful acknowledgement is made to the following publishers:

Bantam Books, Inc., 666 Fifth Avenue, New York, N.Y. 10103, for permission to quote several lines from *The Courage to Live* by Ari Kiev.

Christian Fellowship Publishers, Inc., Box 6302, Silver Springs, Md. 20906, for permission to quote several lines from *The Spiritual Man* by Watchman Nee. Copyright © 1968.

Faith & Life Ministries, Rev. Ernest Rockstad, 632 N. Presperity Lane, Andover, Ks. 67002, for permission to quote several lines from *A Medical Doctor Comments on Mental Illness* by Terry Vanover.

Presbyterian and Reformed Publishing Co., Box 817, Phillipsburg, N.J. 08865, for permission to quote several lines from *Competent to Counsel* by Dr. Jay E. Adams. Copyright © 1970.

Fleming H. Revell Co., 184 Central Avenue, Old Tappan, N.J. 07675, from *None of These Diseases* by S.I. McMillen, M.D., copyright © 1963 by Fleming H. Revell Company. Used by permission.

Saber Publications, P.O. Box 98, Bentley, La., for permission to quote several lines from *Take Heed Brethren Lest* by Conrad Murrell.

The University of Chicago Press, 5801 Ellis Avenue, Chicago, Ill. 60637, for permission to quote several lines from *Spirit, Soul and Flesh* by Ernest DeWitt Burton, 1918.

All possible care has been taken to trace ownership and obtain permission for each quote included. If any errors or omissions have occurred, they will be corrected in subsequent editions, provided they are brought to the publisher's attention.

Contents

CHAPTER 1

The Battleground!

Mental institutions are bursting at the seams, while thriving psychiatrists, psychologists, and marriage counselors have failed to stem the tide. It is common knowledge that probably the majority of patients in general hospitals are suffering primarily from psychological or psychosomatic disorders (that is, suffering caused by mental stress). It has been recently estimated that probably eighty-five percent of all patients in all kinds of hospitals are there because of psychosomatic problems. This indicates strongly that folks are not able to cope with the pressures of everyday life.

It is time to take even a closer look at what is commonly called "mental illness." Could it not be that this ambiguous term is a "misleading misnomer"? That is what the well-known Christian counselor Jay Adams has to say about this term.

> Organic malfunctions affecting the brain that are caused by brain damage, tumors, gene inheritance, glandular, or chemical disorders, validly may be termed mental illnesses. But at the same time, a vast number of other human problems have been classified as mental illnesses for which there is no evidence that they have been engendered by disease or illness at all. As a description of these problems, the term mental illness is nothing more than a figure of speech, and in most cases, a poor one at that.
>
> To put the issue simply: the Scriptures plainly speak of both organically-based problems as well as those problems that stem from sinful attitudes and behavior;

> but where in all of God's Word is there so much as a trace of any third source of problems which might approximate the modern concept of "mental illness"? Clearly, the burden of proof lies with those who loudly affirm the existence of mental illness of disease but fail to demonstrate biblically that it exists. Until such a demonstration is forthcoming, the only safe course to follow is to declare with all of Scripture that the genesis of such human problems is twofold, not threefold.[1]

What then is really wrong with the "mentally ill"? It would seem that the problem is within the individual himself as a result of the fall of Adam. Man is born in sin and has gone astray from his mother's womb "speaking lies" (Psalm 58:3); therefore, he naturally attempts to avoid facing the responsibility of his sin. He fails therefore to make the proper responses when faced with difficult situations. As Dr. Adams states:

> He will fall into varying styles of sin ascending to the short term successes or failures of the particular sinful responses which he makes to life's problems. Apart from organically generated difficulties, the "mentally ill" are really people with unsolved personal problems.[2]

What about the myriads of people who "stuff" our mental institutions? How many folks in these institutions are there because of bona fide, organic, bodily diseases? Dr. Terry Vanover, a physician in Sheppardsville, Kentucky, makes the following observation:

> It is a medical fact that less than three percent of all brain disease or mental disturbances are on an organic basis. In our own personal experience, we have admitted hundreds of patients to the hospital for complete neurological workup and evaluation. After extensive testings, the findings have been examined not only by

[1]Jay E. Adams, *Competent to Counsel* (Nutley: Presbyterian and Reformed Publishing Co., 1970), pp. 28-29.

[2]*Ibid.*

> the family physician, but also by the best specialists in neurology that are available. By far, the majority of these people turn up with findings which are completely normal from the medical point of view.[3]

Dr. Vanover is stating here that the patients who have undergone mental examinations have proven to have little or no physical ailment. This is not to say that they are not feeling ill, but rather no examination has turned up a physical cause. In other words, medical science and those who write the diagnosis on patients do not know what causes these problems. Then he makes an astounding and shocking statement:

> Therefore, it has come to my attention and become my firm belief, having been a Christian for many years, that this is oppression by Satan and that these are the results and manifestations of spiritual assault. In my opinion and in the opinion of many medical doctors, there is no known treatment or lasting cure for that which is diagnosed as schizophrenia, the so-called split personality. I believe that schizophrenia is definitely demonic.[4]

The reader may possibly react to the above conclusion as being rash and irresponsible. However, when we weigh this medical evidence in light of the eternal Word of God, we shall discover the validity of these statements. If these illnesses and disorders are not caused by the organic mind, the physical body or God Himself, then what is their source? This book is an attempt to confront these questions.

Ponder, for instance, the ever-increasing epidemic of suicide in our affluent society. It is estimated that between 25,000 and 50,000 people commit suicide per year in the United States, with the number constantly on the rise.[5]

[3]Terry Vanover, *A Medical Doctor Comments on Mental Illness* (Andover, Faith and Life Publications, n.d.), p. 1.

[4]*Ibid.*

[5]Ari Kiev, *The Courage to Live* (New York: Thomas Y. Crowell Publishers (1979), p. ix.

The number of attempted suicides, moreover, may run as high as 400,000 per year.

It cannot be disputed that young people in the past two decades have had more opportunities afforded them than in any prior time in these United States. Opportunities in education, science, technology, etc., have abounded. Yet it is astounding that in the past twenty years incidents of suicide among young people have increased to epidemic proportions. Paul Harvey recently stated that 13 school-age young people are committing suicide each day!

The ambitious dreams of youth have seemingly been shattered in our generation. It is almost shocking to recognize that suicide among American adolescents is the third most common cause of death, after accidents and homicides. When you add to this the soaring multitude who "cop out" of responsibility by means of alcohol and drugs, the results are staggering.

These facts reveal the tremendous pressure on the minds of the American populous. Despondency, depression, frustration and disillusionment, have all taken their tolls upon young and old alike. The battle is in the minds of men. The Bible states that "as a man thinketh in his heart so is he" (in every area of life). This axiom indicates that a person *is* what he *thinks* and nothing more. The mind controls the man; thus, to have a *mind* under satanic control is to have a *man* under satanic control.

The only answer for man is to have the "mind of Christ"; that is, the indwelling nature of Jesus Christ which comes through saving grace. Therefore, the true believer — the one savingly joined to Christ, is the only one who can think successfully. True biblical success only comes through head and heart action based on and governed by the Word of God (Joshua 1:8).

The saints of God have the supernatural ability to think right (about God, self, sin, etc.), and thus, to live right. However, faulty thinking among believers can lead to the many stresses which plague the unconverted. The church today is filled with neurotic souls who have not learned to "possess their possessions" in Jesus Christ. They have not drawn on His grace and power for daily victory. Consequently, it is not an uncommon thing for even believers to take their own lives.

While few may come to this point, there are many who live on tranquilizers and other artificial means of coping with stress. The time has come to declare war on wrong thinking and the place which believers have given to the world, flesh and the devil in this matter of the mind. Remember, you cannot rise above your thinking process. God has provided for His children a complete armour of protection from the attacks of sin and Satan. Likewise, He has also given us the capacity and ability to think right biblically. It is time that believers appropriate this weaponry and begin anew to "fight the good fight of faith."

In summary, the world is on a collision course. The effects of mental stress, breakdowns and suicides are mounting. Unsolved personal problems are passing off for "mental illness" and the Freudian psychological remedies are coming up short.

There *are* answers, however. God has a solution for every problem facing mankind. He has given us a manual called the Bible which explains where man came from, what he is and what he can be when savingly related by faith to Jesus Christ. There *is* healing for the mind!

CHAPTER 2

The Sick Mind

It has already been established that "mental illness" is a myth. Yet, the mind is sick spiritually because of the fall of man and the resultant curse. There is no hope for us apart from the "healing of the mind."

The first man, Adam, was "fearfully and wonderfully made." He walked in constant fellowship with his Creator. He was robust in every way — physically, mentally and spiritually. The monumental task of naming all of the animals and birds was given to Adam, indicating that he possessed a tremendous mind. The domination of the earth was also delegated to him by God (Genesis 1:28), which suggests Adam's great authority. He was in total subjection to God's will.

Significantly, God tested Adam's love by forbidding him to eat of the "tree of the *knowledge* of good and evil" (Genesis 2:17). This immediately suggests that God desired man's thinking process or mind to be under divine control. Satan knew that if the man was to fall, it would begin within his mind. He *must* get the first couple to think independently of God and His Word. He knew by experience that sin would "hatch" in Adam if he could be tempted to discount Jehovah's Word and become his own god.

Therefore, the subtle serpent moved in on Eve first with "Yea, hath God said . . . ?" He attempted to plant doubt in her mind as to the veracity of God's Word. Satan's strategy has not changed to this day, for the authority and inerrancy of God's Word is still held in question. Eve could have resisted the devil but instead succumbed to the snake's sensuous appeal. Along with Adam, she ate the forbidden fruit. Their "eyes were opened and they *knew* that they were naked." Yes, they thought they had outsmarted God, but were now stripped of His glory and intimate communion. Among other things, their mental and spiritual communication with God was severed. The cancer of sin's curse was now inaugurated among the human race.

While Adam's posterity possessed brilliant minds,[1] the dark depravity of sin was quickly evidenced. We are told that "the wickedness of man was great in the earth and that every imagination of the thoughts of his heart was only evil continually" (Genesis 6:5). The depth of this description is awesome! The word "imagination" (*Yetzer*) means to "form or devise something in the mind." It signifies not only the imagination, but "purposes and desires."[2] Thus, man's *whole* imagination was perverted by sin.

Even more profoundly, "every imagination of his *thoughts (chasheb* — meditations, purposes, plans, etc.)[3] was *only* evil *continually.*" His mind was a total and unending disaster. "The thoughts of his *heart*" being endlessly evil indicates that sin's debauchery was rooted even more deeply in man's spirit — the seat of conscience and spiritual understanding. What a picture of man's total depravity in spirit, soul, and therefore, his body.[4]

Has man's debauched nature ever changed? Let's open the pages of New Testament Scripture and take another look at unregenerate man. Paul states that "the natural man receiveth not the things of the Spirit of God; for they are foolishness unto him . . ." (I Corinthians 2:14). The

[1]Abel was a capable sheepherder (Genesis 4:2). Cain's descendents were skilled in metal and musical instruments (Genesis 4:21-22).

[2]William Wilson, *Old Testament Word Studies* (McLean, Virginia. MacDonald Publishing Co., n.d.), p. 226.

[3]*Ibid.*, p. 444.

[4]See Appendix A. The spirit (boss) affects the soul (foreman) which in turn controls the body's performance (laborer).

man who is "natural" *(psuchikos)* is governed by his soulish or sensuous drives.[5] Since his soul is corrupted by sin, he cannot communicate with God nor understand His thoughts. The "natural" cannot comprehend the spiritual. This is why an unsaved Ph.D. with intellectual excellence cannot receive the plan of salvation in Christ — his mind is in rebellion against God.

More specifically, the New Testament describes the mind as being "reprobate" or incapable of spiritual discernment (Romans 1:28). Here's a mind that has rejected God's light and in turn has been rejected by God. Man thinks *he* is god and indeed, that is the root of his sin.

Paul describes the unregenerate mind as "corrupt" (I Timothy 6:5). This word is translated "destroyed" (Revelation 8:9), and describes the perishing of our mortal bodies (II Corinthians 4:16). What a picture of man's soul! He has been totally destroyed within and without — sin's corruption eating him through and through.[6]

In addition, the Scripture speaks of the "defiled" mind (Titus 1:15). Here is a mind that is stained, polluted and contaminated by sin which vents itself in immoral behavior (see Jude 8). Consider also the "fleshly mind" (Colossians 2:18) which is dominated by man's depraved nature, as opposed to the Holy Spirit's control. The sinner is totally governed by flesh — whether moral, immoral or religious. Jesus said, "that which is born of the flesh is flesh . . ." and cannot possibly be anything else. Thus, a person will never *think* right about anything until he is "born of the Spirit."

Paul, in Ephesians 4:17, exhorts the saints not to walk in the "vanity of the mind" as do unbelievers. Here is the individual who has a misconception of reality, a mind void

[5]*Psuchikos* belongs to *psuche,* "soul (as the lower part of the immaterial in man) . . . relating perhaps . . . to the mind . . . springing from the corrupt desires and affections," W.E. Vine, *An Expository Dictionary of New Testament Words,* 4 vols. (Westwood: Fleming H. Revell Co., 1940), 3:102.

[6]The Greek is intensified, meaning "to corrupt utterly, through and through." *Ibid.,* 1:242.

of true understanding. The word is "foolish, empty" and describes those who exchange the glory of the incorruptible God for corrupted creation (Romans 1:21-23). Indeed, the natural man considers spiritual things foolish because he himself is a fool! In his "vain" mind is lodged a distorted image of the reality of truth. How prevalent is this thinking in our worldly-wise, idolatrous age. Our energies are geared toward our concept of reality. This explains the present clamour for money, pleasure, sex, sports, etc., which never satisfy the soul's thirst for the true God. Driven by a vain and foolish mind, man thinks he's smart, while God calls him a "fool."

A word needs to be said about spiritual blindness. One of the most devastating verses depicting the ungodly mind is Ephesians 4:18: "Having the *understanding* darkened, being alienated from the life of God through the ignorance that is in them, because of the blindness of their hearts."

Notice the shroud of darkness over the mind caused by the spiritual blindness of the heart. The sinner has been cut off from God's life through ignorance, and is therefore devoid of spiritual knowledge. The word "ignorance" stems from our word for "agnostic," meaning "not to know." The natural mind does not know God and therefore suffers the consequence of mere existence, as opposed to abundant life. This is why the rank and file of people act like "yo-yos" going up and down, yet accomplishing nothing of eternal value.

Satan, the god of this world, further takes advantage of man's wicked heart and blinds his mind or mental perception lest he see the light of the Gospel (II Corinthians 4:4). Man in his unregenerate state is doomed — blinded by sin, self and Satan. He is the devil's robot, serving sin with a mind that is "reprobate, corrupt, defiled, carnal, vain and blind"!

Incidentally, each of the above characteristics pertain not to the intellect (soul) primarily, but to the spiritual understanding *(nous)* of men (see Appendix A). What does this mean? It simply means that the innermost core of man — the control center which dictates to his soul and body, is hopelessly devastated by sin.

No wonder Jesus Christ said "Ye *must* be born again"! Thank God, He made a way for divine spiritual life to pierce the sinner's corpse. The entrance of God's Word gives light to the mind "cracked" by matchless grace. Yes, repentance is the answer to a renewed mind in Christ who announced: "Except ye *repent,* ye shall . . . perish" (Luke 13:3). In His great commission to the disciples, Jesus states: "*Repentance* and remission of sin should be preached in my name among all nations."

Why such emphasis on repentance? Because it deals with the sinner's mind — the inner man which controls his attitude and actions. Significantly, repentance is the Greek word *metanoia* meaning "a change of mind." Again, this concerns a divine transformation within man's spiritual understanding (spirit or *nous)* not just a whimsical and fleeting exercise of the brain.

Neither is repentance mere sorrow, for Judas was remorseful over the outcome of his betrayal, yet there was no change of mind or purpose. Herein lies the key to the maladies and sick spirituality of the present-day church. The clarion call to repent is all but unheard, being substituted by a message of "easy believism."[7] No wonder there are so many neurotics, schizophrenics and loonies in our churches! Man today no longer needs to change his mind about God and sin. He need only to "make a decision" for Christ. Don't misunderstand, the sinner is brought to decision by the Holy Spirit in salvation, but not without a radical "change of mind."

In true regeneration, the rebel sinner is *de*throned and the Lord Jesus Christ is *en*throned as King. Only then can one obtain a "renewed mind" (Romans 12:2) which can begin to think right, and thus, generate godly actions. In

[7]By "easy believism," we mean the emphasis of merely "making a decision for Christ" without any repentance for sin and surrender to Christ's Lordship. It is a "gospel" that demands no "newness of life" as a result of conversion.

fact, by repentance one is enabled to hate sin with the same intensity with which he once loved it.

Remember, as a "man thinketh in his heart, so is he." We cannot live higher than we think. That is why the first commandment includes loving God "with all thy *mind*" (Matthew 22:37). God give us a new generation of preachers who will call men to biblical repentance, therefore sparking an epidemic of right thinking.

CHAPTER 3

What About Fear?

Have you ever been afraid? Certainly you have. Was it wrong to be scared? That depends on the situation. Should one not be afraid to enter a dangerous "high voltage" area, or be fearful of stepping too close to the edge of a cliff, or riding the roller coaster with a heart condition? Yes, it is right and natural to be fearful in such circumstances, and this applies to believers and unbelievers alike.

The thrust of this chapter, however, is to seriously consider fear that grips the hearts of God's people living in the midst of a fear-paralyzed society. Security measures and devices for battling uncontrollable crime have fostered a booming business across America. People are afraid to answer their doors or walk on the streets at night. On top of that, most people cannot cope with their personal fears, which accounts for the soaring craze of drug and alcohol consumption. In light of these all-too-familiar problems, has the true church demonstrated God's perfect peace to fear-ridden souls? Have we by example proved to a scared generation that indeed there *is* victory in Jesus? Many will certainly agree that the church of the living God has failed in this important area.

Yet, is it wrong for believers to fear? We have already established that there are natural, safeguard emotions built into all humans for self-preservation purposes. Is there any other legitimate fear? Psychiatrists, psychologists, and even some preachers would say "no"! Even so-called Christian psychologists have argued against the legitimacy of guilt and fear within the Christian. Yet, there *is* a Scriptural basis for fear among the saints — it is called the "fear of God." It ministers proper guilt and conviction which leads one toward repentance.

Solomon says that "the fear of the Lord is the beginning (lit. chief or principal part) of knowledge . . ." (Proverbs 1:7). This is to say that what the ABCs are to reading, the fear of God is to right thinking. In fact, to be devoid of *this* fear is to be rendered stupid, biblically. Without this quality, the astronomer has never really seen a star, nor the physician the true wonder of the body.

Some might argue that the fear of God is an Old Testament concept, certainly not for today. Yet, the New Testament is replete with references and inferences to "the fear of God."[1] Jesus Himself said to the disciples: "Fear not them which kill the body but are not able to kill the soul; but rather fear him which is able to destroy both soul and body in hell" (Matthew 10:28).

Our Lord makes a contrast between the fear of man and the fear of God. Right here is the issue of our discussion. Men fear other men who can only kill the body, rather than fearing God who can cast body *and* soul into Hell! Scripture says that "the fear of man brings a snare" but "the fear of the Lord is the fountain of life" (Proverbs 29:25; 14:27). There is an abundant flow of life in the person who has the right kind of fear.

A key problem today is that people are seized by the wrong fears. In light of this Bible truth, when was the last time you heard a sermon on "Fearing God"? The anemic, lopsided preaching of our day has all but omitted this vital area of truth which potentially could transform the church of God in our generation.

Our counseling rooms are filled with neurotic Christians who have not been counseled properly from the pulpit. Their souls are flooded with fears, stemming from a mental preoccupation with self, Satan and circumstances.

[1]For example, II Corinthians 7:1, Ephesians 5:21, Philippians 2:12, Revelation 14:7, etc.

Without any fear of God and sin, Satan has cleverly blinded our minds through our ignorance of and subsequent disobedience to God's Word. No wonder the church is in such a state of spiritual plight and powerlessness.

What then is the fear of God that keeps us from godless fear? Charles Bridges sights the following definition of the fear of God:

> It is that affectionate reverence by which the child of God bends himself humbly and carefully to his Father's law. His wrath is so bitter and His love so sweet, that hence, springs an earnest desire to please Him and . . . a holy watchfulness and fear "that he might not sin against Him" (Hebrews 12:28-29). This enters into every exercise of the mind, and every object of life.[2]

This may sound like bondage and legalism to some but *this* fear liberates the soul for true worship and service. It recognizes God for what He really is: Jehovah — the Holy One of Israel! He is the One who thundered His law at Sinai and then one day came to earth concealing His eternal glory in human flesh. Yes, the Living Word (Christ) in the New Testament is One with the Old Testament Jehovah! This fact is critical if we are to think properly of God. All of our problems stem from a misconception of the God of Scripture. The mind, out of touch with reality (God) is "sick" and in need of healing grace.

The believer who fears God need not fear. That may sound like double talk, but it is biblically correct. With the Sovereign God in control, what can alarm me? When Israel stood at thundering Mount Sinai, Moses said, "Fear not, for God is come to prove you . . . that *His fear* may be before your faces that you sin not" (Exodus 20:20). Here are two fears — a right and a wrong.

The holy fear of God will create a mind and spirit of awesome worship in the highest level of exercise. There is

[2]Charles Bridges, *An Exposition of Proverbs* (Marshallton: The National Foundation in Christian Education, 1846), pp. 3-4.

a delight in the smile of God along with a corresponding dread of His frown. To seek His favor is the greatest good one can enjoy; to incur His disfavor is the worst of all evils. Jesus put it simply: "If ye love me, keep my commandments and I will pray the Father and He shall give you another Comforter . . ." (John 14:15-16). The Holy Spirit enables us to obey God (right fear) and then comforts our hearts, delivering us from ungodly fears.

What about these unholy fears? Our society is riddled by fear because "there is no fear of God before their eyes" (Romans 3:18). Everyone must fear something or someone. One of Satan's tactics is to blind souls from the fear of God and bind them with ungodly fears. Paul exhorts Timothy — a young, timid preacher, to "stir up"[3] his gift (of power) when faced with fearful opposition. In II Timothy 1:7 he says, "For God hath not given us the *spirit of fear,* but of power, and of love and of a sound mind."

Timothy might have been gripped with a demonic spirit of fear which could have paralyzed his ministry. This was not just natural emotion, but a supernatural invasion of Satan perverting Timothy's capacity to fear. We may not be aware of it, but demons, when given opportunity, can greatly influence our emotions and defeat us spiritually. Sorrow, laughter, anger, etc., are God-given emotions of the soul; yet how often we have seen them carried to unholy extremes. Timothy was under enemy attack, and Paul reminds him of his weapons of warfare.

Christian, if you mean business for God, you are engaged in the oldest, most subtle battle known to man! Satan's tactics have not changed nor decreased. If anything, he has stepped up his campaign because "his time is short." His weapon of slandering God's Word, used so effectively with Adam, has never become obsolete. Satan is bent on capturing our minds — flooding them with fearful doubts, and therefore rendering us powerless.

[3]The Greek word denotes the rekindling or keeping in full flame, a fire that is capable of dying out. Vine, *op. cit.,* 4:75).

Remember, a man is and does what he thinks. The enemy knows this well. Practical instruction in right thinking will be discussed later.

As we progress in grace, our spirit will become increasingly sensitive to inward sin. So often today, spirituality is judged simply on the basis of outward habits (e.g., smoking, cursing, drinking, etc.). A church leader may be selected primarily because these things are absent from his life; yet, the same individual may have a bitter spirit and a slanderous tongue which somehow are not considered serious enough to disqualify him from office. This is not to condone these outward habits (they are wrong), but only to emphasize that sin is internal as well as external.

The point is that one may have victory over external filthiness and yet be imprisoned by soul pollution. You may be a "separated" Christian in dress and outward deportment and yet be worldly in your mind. The Holy Spirit will minister conviction regarding this inconsistency so as to lead you into repentance ("change of mind"); however, if the sin is not properly dealt with, the door is open for Satan's aggravated mental assault (Ephesians 4:27). The only sane remedy is to "cleanse ourselves from all filthiness of the flesh *and* spirit, perfecting holiness in the fear of God" (II Corinthians 7:1). This closes the door to Satan's foothold and opens the door to the blessing and power of God.

But what about attacks of fear that come when you know things are right with God? It is one thing to have Scriptural guilt when becoming sensitive to our sin; it is quite another thing to become overly sensitive, accepting slander and fear in areas where we are not guilty. If Satan cannot blind us to our sin, he will attempt to either slander God's forgiveness to us or create false guilt over non-existent sin. This is the "spirit of fear" and is not from God! A personal testimony will help to illustrate this principle.

Soon after I was converted to Christ, the burden of lost souls gripped my heart. The responsibility to preach the

Gospel to every creature was pressed upon me. I wanted so much to obey God in every area of my life. In the seven-hundred-mile trip from college to my home, there were at least a dozen toll booths stationed on turnpikes and bridges. Somehow, I felt compelled to give a Gospel tract to every toll collector I passed. This seemed spiritual and honoring to God, for I was fulfilling the "great commission." However, an increasing burden developed. If I missed even one collector with a tract, a crippling fear would begin to well up in my chest. I would then beat myself mentally. Of course, I could pass other people by in restaurants, service stations, etc., and all was well. I never realized this inconsistency.

I attributed these fears to the judgment of God because of what I considered failure and disobedience. This became an obsession, whereby I was afraid to pass a toll booth and even thought of traveling the secondary roads. I had no particular burden for any other group of people — just the toll booth collectors! I interpreted this as the "fear of God" for I wanted to obey Him implicitly; yet, I was hung up spiritually over something that should have liberated me.

You see, I found out later that this was a subtle attack of Satan, who slandered my obedience to God; he took something Scriptural like witnessing and made it stereotyped and inflexible. He whispered, "If you don't witness to every toll collector, you don't love God." I wanted to love God supremely, and therefore I had told God I would do anything. Satan picked that up and cleverly drove me to bondage, using a good thing.

The key here is that Satan *drove* me. I discovered later that God is a Shepherd who *leads* His sheep — He doesn't *drive* them (Psalm 23:3). In the "fear of God," He gently burdens our hearts to do His sweet will. The driving or beating force, however, is not from God, but is a spirit of fear, bringing torment to our soul. "Fear has torment," John says, "but perfect love casts out all fear."

To see the distinction between these two fears (the one from God and the other from Satan) was the first step of my deliverance from this enemy attack. Indeed, God had not given me a spirit of fear, but power, love and a sound mind! These principles of II Timothy 1:7 applied by the Holy Spirit brought "healing" to my mind on this and other future occasions. We shall consider some of these truths in succeeding chapters.

CHAPTER 4

Needed: Salvation of the Mind

What a day it was when I became a "new creature" in Christ. Thank God for saving grace that includes a new heart and the forgiveness of sin. But an even greater day registers in my memory when I discovered that my new life in Christ included the potential of a "new head."

The believer's body has become the Holy Spirit's temple or dwelling place (I Corinthians 6:19). More specifically, the Spirit of God has possessed man's spirit in salvation (Romans 8:16). As Watchman Nee says:

> Man's spirit is the place where man works together with God. How do we know that we have been born anew and are therefore children of God? We know because our inner man has been quickened and the Holy Spirit dwells therein. Our spirit is a regenerated, renewed one, and He Who dwells in, yet is distinct from, this new spirit is the Holy Spirit. And the two of them bear witness together.[1]

This is illustrated in type by the Holy of Holies of the Old Testament temple, where Jehovah's glorious presence dwelled. The innermost part of the temple pictures our spirit from which the Holy Spirit influences our soul and body (see Appendix A).

When God gave the blueprint of the Tabernacle to Moses, He began with the Ark in the Holy of Holies and proceeded to the outside gate. Significantly, God begins His saving work in man's spirit (heart) and progresses out-

[1]Watchman Nee, *The Spiritual Man*, 3 vols (New York: Christian Fellowship Publishers, Inc., 1968), 2:16-17.

wardly through the soul and body. On the other hand, man's religion always begins on the *outside,* attempting to eventually change the inside. Thus religion majors in external "do's and don'ts," being incapable of changing man's heart. Salvation, on the other hand, is a divine invasion of God's Spirit into man's spirit, resulting in inward and outward godliness. A city rescue mission once advertised, "We don't put a new suit on the man, but we put a new man in the suit." Well said!

Is it possible then to have a new head or mind even though salvation is primarily a heart matter? Indeed, God has made provision in grace for the whole man. He has granted us not only power and love, but a "sound mind" (II Timothy 1:7). The Greek root word here *(sophroneo)* literally means the "saving of the mind." What a tremendous thought it is that redemption includes the salvation or deliverance of our minds.

It is necessary, however, to understand that while the believer's spirit is presently and totally redeemed, the soul and body *are being* redeemed. According to Romans 8:23, the believer's body, while presently dying, awaits a full and future redemption (deliverance). Yet, God's saving grace has made provision for physical healing today[2] even though our bodies will eventually succumb to the grave.

Likewise, Scripture indicates that our souls (mind, emotion and will) are yet to be fully redeemed. Peter, for instance, instructs us that after the present tribulation and temptations of this earthly life we shall behold our God, receiving then "the salvation of our souls" (I Peter 1:9). This is not to say that a believer isn't saved now, but rather there is a consummation or completeness of our salvation yet future in Glory.

James commands the Christians to put away "all filthiness . . . and receive with meekness the engrafted word, which is able to save your souls" (James 1:21). The context here is one of obedience — being "doers of the Word and

[2]See Exodus 15:26, Matthew 8:17, James 5:14f.

not hearers only." Yes, the soul moving in the fear of God is being saved (delivered). That means the believer can walk in the victory of Jesus Christ, having his mind, emotions and will under God's control. This is the present aspect of salvation.

To express it another way, the believer *has been* saved from the penalty of sin (justification); he *is being* saved from the power of sin (sanctification); and by God's grace, he *shall be* saved from the very presence of sin (glorification). Yes, it *is* possible to have a mind that is functioning right now for the glory of God.

Why are there so many depressed, pill-popping Christians today? In answer to this, let us consider again the powerful implications of II Timothy 1:7. Rather than tolerating a "spirit of fear," the believer has been graced with the Spirit who grants power, love and soundness (saving) of the mind. But this fact must be known *and* appropriated by the child of God. You cannot effectively latch on to something that you know nothing about. How many times I tolerated mental depression and fear because I didn't realize what was mine in Christ. Millions of Christians who are constantly plagued with subtle satanic attacks on the mind are ignorant of the fact and reality that there *is* salvation of the mind. We can have a victorious thought life, by the grace of God.

You may wonder about the insane and so-called "mentally ill" who fill our institutions and walk the streets. Is there any hope for them? Significantly, Jesus confronted a maniac near Galilee (Luke 8:26f) who had been demonized for a long time. Luke says that he "had devils" (Lit. *daimonia* — "demons") while Mark states that he had "an unclean spirit" (5:2). This man fits the description of what is commonly called "demon possession" and yet Jesus healed him.

Let's consider the evidence of healing grace in the former lunatic. When the demons had left him at Christ's command, he was found "sitting at the feet of Jesus, clothed, and in his right mind" (Luke 8:35). Please note that "right mind" is the Greek word *sophroneo* translated "sound mind" in II Timothy 1:7. The maniac was not only delivered from demons ("spirit of fear") and joined to Christ, but experienced salvation of the mind. Think of it, a demon-possessed man is completely saved, including the healing of his mind! Mentally deranged at one time, he is now capable of thinking logically, soberly and spiritually.

Can Jesus Christ do the same today for so-called insane and mentally deranged people? If He can't, then the Gospel is *not* the "power of God unto salvation" and we Christians have nothing to preach. Moreover, we ourselves are lost, for it took no less power to save us than it did to convert the maniac. What encouragement and hope this holds out for a world of "insane" people.

We need to take a closer look at insanity and demonic control. It is possible to view the man of Gadara as some unique case. One might gleefully exclaim, "I'm glad I wasn't insane and demonically controlled when Christ found me." Don't be too sure! We were "of our father the devil" (John 8:44), and ever since conversion bouts have been fought with satanic doubts, fears and depressions. Since our minds are not yet completely redeemed, we can still "give place to the devil" (Ephesians 4:27) if we are not walking in the fear of God.

Let us consider some of the symptoms evidenced in the demon-controlled man prior to his conversion. Luke tells us that he wore no clothes; that is, he had a propensity toward nudity. We are told that this is very prevalent among patients in mental hospitals. However, nudity is openly relevant to our day of fleshly displays in movies, magazines and television. During the driving beat of a rock concert, some people have been known to remove their clothes. False religions and the occult are often replete with sexual overtones. Lust and sensuality have even crept their way into evangelicalism via music, films and books.

The key factor here is that this man was "driven of the

devil'' (Luke 8:29). We said earlier that Satan always *drives* his subjects, and thereby we can detect the source of our mental burden. Note that ''Jesus . . . was *led* by the Spirit'' (Luke 4:1) and so is every child of God (Romans 8:14). The Lord is our Shepherd King who leads us beside the waters of quietness — He doesn't drive us to despair. How many times believers have been frightfully driven to do the ''will of God'' only to be left in a state of frustration. To this day, they think God was leading, when in reality, it was Satan driving. How wonderful it is to discover God's sweet leading, for ''His yoke is easy and His burden is light.''

The demoniac was not only naked but anti-social, living ''in the tombs.'' Obviously, he could not rightly relate to other people and was preoccupied with death. This problem is not unique to insane people. Our world (and church) is filled with insecure, fear-driven, morbid people. No, not to the same excess as the demoniac, but still preoccupied to some degree with death rather than life.

Mark depicts this man as being restless and destitute, ''crying and cutting himself with stones.'' This vividly indicates his depression and suicidal tendencies. Certainly, these are very prevalent and real to many so-called ''sane'' people today. We may not literally cut ourselves, but certainly the human race is bent on destroying itself. Our addictions, for example, like smoking, drinking, gluttony, etc., are whittling away our life span. The demoniac was ''bound with chains'' (Luke 8:29) literally, but how descriptive that is of the mastery of sin in anyone's life.

Certainly, if the sinner's spiritual father is the Devil, then he is under Satan's control. Matthew speaks of Jesus healing those who were ''possessed with devils'' (Matthew 4:24). The word used here is *daimonizomai,* rendered ''demonized.'' The phrase ''demon-possession'' is not used per se in the New Testament. This fact is most significant, for it suggests that demonizaton is a matter of *degrees.*

Every soul without God is demonized to one extent or another. Satan can demonstrate his power openly and excessively as in the maniac; but he also moves subtly and quietly as in the case of the false cultist who has been demonically hypnotized. Satan either demonstrates his power openly in competition with God, or he moves incognito so as to give the impression that he doesn't exist. For instance, spiritualists and witch doctors openly practice their occult in South America; we in North America are mesmerized by materialism and flesh under which Satan hides. Some people "blow their stacks" openly while others "stew" quietly — what's the difference? Would it not be legitimate to conclude that because of sin's depravity there are seeds of "insanity" in everyone?

Is not every saint under some degree of demonic control when he gives place to the devil? To whatever extent we let Satan control us, it is just to that extent that we are "demonized." We may not appreciate that terminology, but we need to take another hard look at the truth in light of our depravity. The soul's saturation with the Word of God is therefore essential to insure spiritual victory and effectiveness. As Christians, we need to be more serious about this matter of walking with God.

What about King David who permitted a string of sins (adultery, lying, murder, etc.), to drive him to despair?[3] When Peter rejected our Lord's prediction of His crucifixion, why did Christ say "Get behind me Satan!"? Who was Jesus talking to? Evidently, Peter was momentarily under satanic control and Jesus addressed the serpent himself. In fact, Jesus made it clear to Peter that Satan desired to bind him and "sift him as wheat" (Luke 22:31).

How cocky and glib Christians are today who presume that because they've "been saved" that life is just a smooth ride into the sunset. Yes, there *is* victory in Jesus Christ, but not without battle. Peter himself tells us to "be sober, be vigilant, because your adversary, the devil, as a roaring lion walketh about seeking whom he may devour." He knew firsthand what he was saying.

[3]Read Psalm 32 and 51.

Some may accuse this writer of looking for demons under every bush. God forbid! The point is, that God has given the believer a sound (saved) mind that must be utilized by faith against the aggression of Hell. Since our bodies and souls are not completely redeemed, we are still plagued with disease and mental anguish. We must never blame God *or* Satan for our defeats — the problem is with *us.* Disobedience and unbelief will always lead to our downfall. Regardless of what the ungodly "trinity" (world, flesh and the Devil) throws at us, we have the whole armour of God to protect us. We must not let our emotions, mind and will be controlled by anyone except the Lord Jesus Christ — the Helmet of Salvation. This, however, is probably the vital problem area in the contemporary church. We shall consider later our spiritual resources necessary to win the battle of the mind.

CHAPTER 5

Mental Depression: Satan's Choice Weapon

Thank God for salvation that produces a sound mind. What a comfort it is to know that we can now *think* right in Christ, and thus *be* right. What about the many who are plagued with doubts, discouragement and depression? What causes our mental problems? How far down can a person go in his depression? Is it possible for a Christian to commit suicide? Is there a cure for depression? We shall attempt to face squarely the matter of mental depression in this chapter.

First of all, it is necessary to establish the premise that all of our problems are theologically based, that is, they have some relationship between us and the God who made us. This vertical relationship (God and man) was destroyed by Adam's sin, thus necessitating man's reconciliation through the blood of Christ. Because of sin, God's thoughts are not our thoughts, and therefore, only by saving grace can a man think rightly (biblically) of God.

To be saved or rightly related to God results in a right horizontal relationship (man to man). Our understanding of God will in turn affect our understanding of ourself and others around us. When Isaiah, for instance, gazed upon the glory of God, he cried, "Woe is me for I am undone; because I am a man of unclean lips and I dwell in the midst of a people of unclean lips" (Isaiah 6:5). He saw himself and others in proper perspective when he had a proper concept of Jehovah. So it is with us.

Modern psychological systems emphasize this horizontal (man to man) relationship, but deny by concept and/or practice the vertical (God to man) relationship. It is right here that humanistic psychology and psychiatry fail. Only the Bible offers the dogmatic standard upon which man's actions can be tested. Evolutionary and humanistic theories leave man in the dark as to his origin, his future destiny and his present dilemma. God made man and gave him an infallible Manual (God's Word) to guide him from earth to heaven. Who can better analyze and assist man than the One who created him?

Who better understands an automobile, for instance, than the one who designed it? For that reason, the manufacturer supplies a manual of instruction for the consumer to follow. How often do people disregard instructions and take things into their own hands only to devastate the product. Their philosophy can be stated as follows: "When all else fails, read the directions." That actually sums up the theory of most people who play havoc with their eternal soul and never "read the instructions" that God — the designer — has provided for our total well-being.

Unfortunately even God's people disregard the Manual (Bible) and therefore suffer the same basic defeats experienced by those of the world. This is nothing new, even among the saints recorded in Scripture. Depression or dejection gripped men like Job, David, Elijah and Jeremiah for varying periods of time. Study their lives and find that the root of their problem was unbelief or a distorted view of God. What they thought of God had great bearing on what they thought of themselves. Elijah, for instance, who called the fire down from Heaven on Mount Carmel, was the same prophet who, soon after, cowered in a cave at Beersheba totally disheartened. What made the difference? On the mount, he had his mind focused on the omnipotent God; in the cave, his vision was limited to his own impotence and fearsome circumstance.

I doubt that any child of God in any age has escaped the monster of depression. One cannot appreciate the depression Psalms of David (e.g., Psalm 5, 6, 10, 13, etc.) until he's been depressed. Thank God for the "salvation of the mind" which can and must be appropriated through God's Word in times of discouragement and trial. The men of God mentioned above eventually found release and victory as they dealt with their unbelieving mental attitudes.

However, if a Christian is not careful in dealing Scripturally with his discouragement, the enemy will take advantage of him and drive him to despair. There are many saints of God who today are rendered helpless because they have not dealt properly with their souls. The church is filled with so-called "nervous Christians" on the verge of a mental breakdown; poor souls who are emotionally high-strung and have lost all spiritual sanity. They could well be called "unbelieving believers." How pathetic and yet true.

A solemn word of warning and exhortation is in order for every child of God. Satan is out to devour (chew up) every Christian and render him powerless (I Peter 5:8). If the reader is not saved, then Satan has you already. The next best thing is to paralyze the one who finally comes to Christ so that he cannot experience the fulness of God's salvation. For example, let's consider in brief the life of King Saul and the events that contributed to his prolonged depression and his tragic death.

At the outset, some may object to the inference that Saul was a believer. Certainly we cannot be dogmatic, but there are several facts to indicate that he belonged to God. First, Saul was chosen and called of the Lord to reign over Israel (I Samuel 9:15f). Second, he was anointed as king by Samuel (I Samuel 10:1); third, God gave him another heart (10:9); and fourth, the "Spirit of God came upon him and he prophesied" (10:10). Frankly, I don't know of any place in all of Scripture where these things happened to an unregenerate man. The evidence seems to favor that Saul was indeed a converted man, though obviously motivated so frequently by the flesh.

Saul had a good start like so many believers. Scripture indicates that he was humble and admirably assumed his God-given responsibility. In time, however, he becomes lax in his commitment to God's commands and begins a downhill course of disobedience. Let each of us search his heart and learn from the experience of a king who got into trouble because he didn't think right.

Saul's spiritual descent begins in the midst of conflict with the Philistines (I Samuel 13). He has just won a victory over a garrison of enemy troops. The Philistines are now gathered in full array bringing fear to Saul and his men. Samuel, the priest, was on his way to encourage the army of Israel by offering a burnt sacrifice to God in their behalf. When Samuel didn't come on the appointed day, the king decided to take things into his own hands; he offered the sacrifice himself, thus usurping the priest's office. This was a direct violation of God's command. Ironically, Saul had no sooner finished offering the sacrifice when Samuel came and rebuked him openly.

The sin "found him out" immediately and all because Saul *thought* God would overlook his transgression. Here lies a basic problem faced by every Christian — we justify our disobedience because of the circumstance. It seemed innocent on the surface, as sin so often does, but Saul's action demonstrated faulty thinking. The Lord's authority was being desecrated before a nation. Saul's motive was admirable but his method was abominable to God. This seems harsh to our depraved mind, does it not, for certainly the "end justifies the means" — or does it? This was the same reasoning that got us into the original "mess" through Adam and Eve. Sin's thinking has not changed one iota in all of human history!

There is no indication that Saul repented of his deed, and thus did not correct his thinking about God or sin. This fact is critical if we are to understand Saul's tragic end. It is also critical if we are to understand why believers are so mentally depressed and defeated.

God is holy. That is, He loves the right and hates the wrong. Thus God says to His creation: "Be ye holy, for I am holy." A righteous man therefore will love what God loves and hate what God hates. His desire is to walk in the fear of God, or to please (obey) his heavenly Father. Saul made the wrong choice and did foolishly, thus losing his kingdom (I Samuel 13:13f).

The child of God is reigning in Christ, but every time he sins, that reigning power (mentally, emotionally, etc.) is temporarily lost until he repents. Saul's greatest problem here was the failure to repent and make things right with God and Israel. Mark it down, depression seeds are planted when we permit our minds to be controlled by a sinful thought pattern. Remember, repentance is a "change of mind" about our sin and about what God says about our sin.

The narrative of Saul progresses as he continues to war against the Philistines with apparent success, *in spite of* his previous disobedience. It is important that Saul not become presumptuous, thinking he is right because of external success in battle. Nor should any man thus presume on God, for built into His mercy is the outpouring of His goodness which should lead us to repentance. However, in Saul's case this did not happen. Significantly, he attempts to seek counsel of God concerning the battle, but God "answered him not that day" (14:37). Scripture makes clear that God will not answer those who harbor sin in their hearts.*

God sends the king a message through Samuel to completely destroy the Amalekites and all their possessions (I Samuel 15). These were the enemies of God and His people. These people typify the flesh, which is always subject to God's judgment and death. Again Saul is put to the test of obedience to God's Word, and again he flunks the test. Instead of wiping out the Amalekites completely, he spares their king and the best of the animals.

*See Psalm 66:18, Proverbs 28:13, I John 3:22.

When confronted by Samuel, Saul has the audacity to say piously, "Blessed be thou of the Lord; I have performed the commandment of the Lord" (15:13). Meanwhile, the presence of Agag and the bleating of the sheep, etc., contradict Saul's statement. After all, he had destroyed *almost* all of the Amalekites, saving only the best for God's purposes.

Saul reasoned that God would accept *partial* obedience to His clear command if he had a "spiritual" motive for not obeying completely. Thinking he could offer the best animals for sacrifices to the Lord, he spared them. God wasn't interested in the Amalekites' best (flesh) for sacrifice, and neither is He desirous of the sanctified flesh offered Him today by a worldly church. So much of what assumes the appearance of true Christianity in these days is prompted by the flesh and not the Spirit. Many of God's servants have sincere motives, but have side-stepped the clear precepts of God's Word. Yes, the flesh must die and give rise to that which is spiritual (Scriptural).

Samuel's rebuke to Saul echoes down to the present: "To obey is better than sacrifice, for rebellion is as the sin of witchcraft and stubbornness is as iniquity and idolatry. . . !" Saul *thought* what he did was right, but it is always wrong to do wrong even if you think something right will come out of it. It is wrong to disobey God in order to obey Him. "Shall we sin that grace may abound?" asks Paul. The answer: "God forbid!"

Remember the point of our discussion is that Saul's mental concept of God's command was faulty, leading to sin's deception, deceit, and depression. What he *thought* was right, in reality was wrong! Here is a believer who placed his mind above the Word of God and thereby lost his kingship. That is exactly what Lucifer and Adam did prior to the fall. What a lesson then in human pride, which led to highmindedness and what God calls "witchcraft and idolatry." Certainly Saul's thoughts were not God's thoughts, and except for God's divine grace, neither are ours.

There is evidence in this narrative that Saul experienced remorse for his sin but never repented. The result was a loss of God's holy anointing, replaced by an "evil spirit" that terrified him (16:14). We see here another consequence of disobedience — great fear which left him depressed. It is important to note here that Saul's sin didn't just create loss of fellowship with God, which is horrible enough, but opened the way for satanic attack.

Many believers today glibly speak of sin as merely a breach of fellowship with God, as though it is nothing to be concerned about. Again, our mental attitude toward God's character and Word is perverted, giving way to a cheap grace. Sin is a tragedy to a believer, for God has made provision for us not to sin (I John 2:1).

No, I do not hold to what some call "sinless perfection," but neither do I condone the prevalent attitude that grace grants a license to sin. Quite the contrary; grace gives us *liberty* to *do right!* Saul got bound up spiritually because of an unrepentant heart that tried to out-think God. We shall analyze this episode more carefully in the next chapter.

Thus far we have watched Saul's downhill course, from losing his reigning power, to being terrified by a demon. In chapter 17, he is confronted with Goliath and the Philistine army. His defeated and now oppressed mind (and soul) leaves Saul paralyzed in facing the giant. Oh, how this speaks to the backslidden believer who is utterly powerless when confronted by the adversary. Thank God that David (type of Christ) finally stepped in and killed the giant, winning the victory for Israel.

Certainly this should have led Saul to repentance. But instead he persisted in his rebellion. Now he becomes jealous of David who has won the nation's respect as a man of God. He envies one who is more godly than himself. Is this not what happens to depressed believers today as well? In fact, this jealous spirit becomes so severe that

Saul attempts to take David's life (18:10-11). It must be noted that when jealousy rages, we can kill people in our minds without throwing a javelin as did Saul. The king is now mentally deranged, driven by the enemy of his soul.

How horrible is this progression of events, and the worst is yet to come. We find this benighted king groping in the depressive darkness of despair. He is looking for light and wisdom but there is no message from God. The communication line has been cut by persistent sin, and Saul in desperation turns to a witch for advice (I Samuel 28). How utterly ironic for the man chosen of God to stoop so low. His rebellion was called "witchcraft," and now he actually involves himself personally with a witch. Oh, the utter folly and devastation of sin!

The reader may think this course of events impossible for a true believer. Yet how many believers today who once had a radiant testimony, are groping in the darkness of depression. It would be interesting to candidly know their thoughts and the experience which they have shared with King Saul. In this frame of mind, the Bible becomes just a book of words — God stops speaking. You begin to pray, but there is no audience with God. The next step is to find an individual that may help. Instead of contacting someone who knows God and His Word, the dejected saint runs to a godless psychiatrist or counselor. Not finding help, he may revert to astrology, a fortune teller or spiritualist (witch) for answers.

Yes, these kinds of people are sitting in church pews. They need a message from God that there *is* salvation and healing of the mind in Jesus Christ! There *is* victory over depression! One *can* live a normal, spirit-filled life in Christ! The Word of God has the answer for *every* need of man — but somehow Saul missed it.

How exhilarating it would be to have Saul's life end in triumph — appropriating God's delivering power from sin and destruction. This is not the case, however. In fact, this king, who refused to repent of his rebellion, was eventually driven to suicide (I Samuel 31:4). He continued so far in disobedience that when wounded in the midst of his last battle, he fell upon his own sword.

What a tragic ending of a man who had been called, anointed, and enthroned by God Almighty. Christian, let us deal stringently with our sin, appropriating the grace of God, lest we follow a similar downhill trek to defeat and despair. It *can* happen to us too. But thanks be to God, He has provided the believer with His "whole armour" for protection in spiritual combat. We shall consider the principles of warfare in a later chapter.

This chapter reminds us that while God has made full provision for a life of victory in Christ, we must mentally and spiritually appropriate that victory. We must think right about God's plan for us as revealed in the Word and set out to fulfill it. Saul failed here — we must not! Yet remember, if failure comes we do have an Advocate with the Father — Jesus Christ the righteous one (I John 2:1). There is forgiveness through Christ when confession is made (I John 1:9). Don't delay as Saul did. We need not live in mental depression.

To the reader who has never trusted Christ for his soul salvation, I urge you to flee to Christ today. Receive Him as the Lord and Saviour of your life. Your mental depression will be swallowed up by His overcoming power and grace.

CHAPTER 6

What About the Mind and Demonic Oppression?

Though we have just concluded a discussion on the subject of depression, the word itself is not used in Scripture. Certainly its characteristics of melancholy, discouragement, dejection, etc., are clearly illustrated as in the life of Saul. However, it is significant that when Christ came, it is said by Peter that "God anointed Jesus of Nazareth with the Holy Ghost and with power; who went about doing good, and healing all that were oppressed of the devil; for God was with him" (Acts 10:38).

The ministry of Jesus Christ included the healing of people "oppressed of the devil." What does this word "oppressed" mean? While depression has the root idea of "to press down or lower," the meaning of oppression is "to exercise power over another." The word used in Acts 10:38 means "to exercise harsh control or power over one." These people were being constantly held under the tyranny of Satan's power.[1]

Funk and Wagnall's Dictionary defines oppression as "to burden or to keep in subjection by harsh and unjust use of force or authority." It also has the sense of a weight pushing down, overwhelming one either physically or mentally. It seems that oppression is extremely intense *de*pression caused by some degree of control over the person.

A similar word *kataponeo,* is used in the account of Israel's oppression in Egypt (Acts 7:24). It means to "ex-

[1]The verb here is a present passive participal construction, *katadunasteuomenous,* indicating continual oppression brought to bear by another force (passive).

haust a person with labor; hence to afflict or oppress." Peter uses it to describe the soul of Lot who was "vexed" (oppressed) by the wickedness of Sodom (II Peter 2:7). Thus, we can deduct that oppression is first self-induced by disobedience (e.g., Lot, Saul, etc.); then, Satan (or his demons) has opportunity to subjugate that one to his harsh tyranny.

One may argue that the folks healed of demonic oppression were all unsaved people. That may possibly be true, but Satan does not give up just because folks get saved. Thank God, Satan's power was broken at the Cross and the believer *can* be an overcomer through Christ. However, Satan continues to attack us mentally and physically. If the Christian gives him place by disobedience, then there is no telling how far the taskmaster of hell will go. We are secured in Jesus Christ and shall never be repossessed by Satan. Yet, great care must be given to be filled with God's Word, for that which is not committed to God is potentially a target of the enemy. We must, therefore, appropriate by faith the "*whole* armour of God."

In Saul's case, we have witnessed a demonic invasion of his mind, replacing the previous anointing of God's Spirit. What a horrible thought, and yet the fact stares us in the face. We shall not argue as to whether Saul was indwelt by a demon at this time. Much is being written pro and con these days on the possibility of a believer being indwelt by demons. To engage in this argument is not our purpose here. Suffice to say that King Saul was under demonic control. Whether the spirit operated from within or without of Saul's body is irrelevant at this point. The issue we must face is that he was oppressed of the Devil, and that somehow, if that can happen to Saul, it can also happen to a believer today.

The saint who insists on walking in the flesh (i.e., under sin's control) instead of the Spirit, gives satanic spirits opportunity to intensify the natural tendencies of the flesh. Wicked desires will be manifested in supernatural jealousies, lusts, angers, adulteries, hatreds, envies, etc. "This is what happened to Saul," says Conrad Murrell, "and God had it recorded for our instruction and admonition." He further states:

> All the way through the remainder of Saul's life we find this evil spirit coming upon him, twisting and surpassing his natural desires, captivating and compelling him to do that which even he is not evil enough to do. This constantly tormented his soul, reducing him to a miserable wretch who could not master his own actions, let alone manage a kingdom.[2]

Mr. Murrell refers to Saul's condition as "demonic obsession." We have discussed mental depression and oppression, but what is "obsession"? Like the word depression, this term is not used in Scripture per se, and yet its characteristics are clearly seen. Obsession comes from the verb meaning "to occupy or trouble the mind to an excessive degree"; to harass, haunt or vex. It is used in psychiatry for an "unwanted or compulsive idea or emotion persistently coming to awareness." It might be called an oppression or captivation which specifically involves the mind.

This seems to pinpoint Saul's dilemma, for his mind seemed to be possessed with unwanted and wicked thoughts. It is well to know that an unregenerated man wants to sin, while the child of God desires righteousness instead of sin. This fact may further verify that Saul was a believer, driven at this point by a demon rather than being led by the Holy Spirit. This is very solemn, and has tremendous implications to those who hold a cheap view of eternal security (i.e., "I'm saved, and it makes no difference how I live").

The church today is quick to quote John 10:28 where Jesus said, "I give unto them eternal life; and they shall never perish, neither shall any man pluck them out of my

[2]Conrad Murrell, *Take Heed Brethren Lest . . .*(Zachary: Fires of Revival Publishers, n.d.), p. 160.

hand." What a glorious truth, and yet to whom is He speaking? The previous verse states "my sheep hear my voice and I know them and they follow me." He is talking to His "sheep" — the people whom He knows in grace; and these sheep *hear* (heed) His voice (Word) and *follow* (obey) Him!

This promise is only for believers, and believers are folks who are bent on following God. Too many have made the term "eternal security" a cliche, unwittingly advocating a license to sin rather than gracious liberty to serve. This belief is not mere profession but possession of Christ, who alone can secure us. As the Puritans of old expressed, "There is no preservation of the saints without perseverance of the saints." They were *not* advocating the possibility of "falling from grace," but simply stating Paul's principle of "*working out* your own salvation with fear and trembling; for it is God who *worketh in* you both to will and to do of His good pleasure." We work out what God works in! True believers have a new heart which gravitates to God's truth, and they endure to the end by the same grace that brought them originally into the Kingdom.

As in Saul's case, every child of God is engaged in warfare, though divinely secured. There is no promise of an easy road in this life, even though we are in the Father's hand. Thus Saul received God's anointing in preparation for this spiritual combat, but he forfeited this blessing through disobedience. Mark it down, there is always a reason why a Christian is powerless. Either he has never been filled with the Holy Spirit, or he has lost the fulness because of sin.

Saul vividly portrays the defeated Christian who has opened himself to the Devil. Whole churches are in this condition today, playing the religious game under demonic oppression. What a tragedy that we have failed to possess our possessions in Christ, as did the early church who moved in resurrection power. Those flaming evangels cashed their spiritual checks and appropriated the blessing of Pentecost. They were victors rather than victims. The need of the hour is for the church to shake loose of its lethargy and despair, and become "more than conquerors" once again!

But how can such deliverance come when one has been ensnared by sin and Satan? Was there hope for Saul? Is there hope for oppressed souls today? Scripture has already announced that the "Son of God was manifested that He might destroy the works of the devil" (I John 3:8). He did not come to start a new religion, for religious activity abounded in His day. In fact, it was religious people that crucified Him. No, He came to "save (deliver) His people from their sin." He came that we might have life "more abundantly" (John 10:10), and to make that possible He "snapped" Satan's power!

The awesome depth of Christ's ministry is certainly beyond our comprehension. The crippling effect of the fall is so encompassing and extensive that only God through His Son could correct it. Let us, therefore, give unceasing praise and adoration to the glorious person and victory of our Lord Jesus Christ! Let us be caught up with *Him* alone, yielding nothing to the enemy of our souls.

Yet, in light of our redeemed position in Christ, why are we not more enamored with our Saviour and more victorious over the world, the flesh and the devil?[3] Could it be that to one degree or another we may be self-deceived or demonized by the enemy? It is altogether tenable that our minds are subconsciously focusing on lies rather than truth. We must be "deprogrammed" from untruth and programmed constantly by the Word of God (Psalm 119:11). Let anyone beware who claims that he could never be deceived, for such a boast indicates that he is already deceived. Just as every man has a physical blind spot where the retina of the eye meets the optic nerve, so every man has spiritual blind spots or areas where he can-

[3]The unholy "trinity" which opposes the believer as a unit.

not see. This is why we need every member of the body of Christ, for no one person sees it all. We must "exhort one another daily . . . lest any of you [us] be hardened through the deceitfulness of sin" (Hebrews 3:13).

God forbid that any child of God become "cocky" in this area of demonic deception and oppression. As has previously been demonstrated, many of God's choice servants besides Saul suffered under Satan's ruthless tyranny. To the best of our knowledge, deliverance came to these men as they dealt with their sin (e.g., Elijah, David, etc.).

However, we find that in no instance did God's servants ever "breeze through" life, even in their sunset years. David, for example, paid dearly for his disobedience even after God released him from oppression. The study of David's life is almost anti-climactic and depressive; for even after his adulterous episode, the fruit of his sin was evidenced in his family, causing constant heartache and unrest. Yet, this is the great King David who was "a man after God's own heart"!

But you say, "These men were in the Old Testament dispensation and thus, did not have the Holy Spirit's power and victory as in the church today." We must remind ourselves, however, that New Testament saints like Peter, Timothy and myriads of those recorded in church history suffered from the hand of the same enemy. Even our Lord Jesus Christ tasted the oppressing power of Satan in Gethsemane, when God permitted His Son to be "touched with the feelings of our infirmities." The pressure was so great that He began sweating drops of blood.

Could it be that every demon of Hell converged on the scene as Christ bore our load of sin? Some commentators suggest this. One thing is sure, Christ destroyed him that had the power of death, that is the Devil! Therefore, the way of victory has been secured for the children of God.

This writer has known of choice soldiers of the Cross — men mightily used of God, who have succumbed to great depression and satanic attack. Some of these same individuals have even taken their own lives in suicide. We do not know why God permits such things except to demonstrate: 1) That it was God's grace alone that enabled them to serve God effectively; 2) No servant of Christ can ever presume on God's goodness — he must always be strong in the Lord and in the power of His might; and 3) That to God alone be the glory for whatever was accomplished.

Thank God there *is* deliverance from Satan's grip. While some have experienced it, others have not. Saul had the same anointing by the Holy Spirit as did David and the Apostle Paul. God's victory certainly is retroactive in relation to the Cross, for God's delivering power has always been operative in any age. Let us consider further what happened in Saul's situation.

The primary step for God's forgiveness and deliverance is repentance or change of mind about sin and God. Saul never took that step; herein is the difference with David, who was quick to repent before the Lord. Some believers are more stubborn than others, who eventually by their persistence will commit "the sin unto death" (I John 5:16) and be taken out of the world (e.g., Saul, Ananias and Sapphira, etc.).

Scripture says that "the spirit of the Lord departed from Saul and an evil spirit from the Lord troubled [literally terrified] him" (I Samuel 16:14). Note that the evil spirit was "from the Lord"; it was sanctioned or permitted by God. Even the Devil himself can't move without God's sovereign permission! Yet God allowed it in spite of all who might cry, "That's not fair." It is time for the church *and* the world to acknowledge the true and living God who reigns supremely in Heaven. We need to experience the doxology of King Nebuchadnezzar who after being divinely delivered from despair proclaimed:

> He doeth according to His will in the army of heaven and among the inhabitants of the earth; and none can

stay His hand, or say unto Him, what doest thou? (Daniel 4:35).

While Saul did not experience a full deliverance, there were times of refreshing and release through David's music ministry. Significantly, David was now God's choice to succeed Saul over Israel. David, being now anointed of God, had a Spirit-filled ministry of music. His godliness was recognized by Saul's servants who likewise discerned Saul's demonic oppression.

> And it came to pass when an evil spirit from God was upon Saul, that David took a harp and played with his hand; so Saul was refreshed and was well and the evil spirit departed from him (I Samuel 16:23).

As David played and praised God, the evil spirit had to leave and Saul was refreshed. The Hebrew word here conveys the idea of "easy breathing." Anyone familiar with demonic oppression knows the heaviness in the chest and the corresponding difficulty in breathing. This was temporarily released when the demon backed off.

At least two factors in this incident are vital to our study. First, the demonic spirit was able to bring physical discomfort to Saul. His spiritual condition had great bearing on his physical well-being. This principle will be discussed in the next chapter.

Second, the ministry of praise through David, brought release and refreshment from oppression. Had Saul taken the first step of repentance, this release from the evil spirit may have been complete and final. Yet, this demonstrates the power of praise in demonic deliverance. Here David effectively ministered to Saul, but how tremendous the result had Saul been able to praise God himself.

The believer who has fallen into mental and spiritual depression must remember the prominent place of praise in running off the enemy. Praise is faith in action, standing on the finished work of Christ.

When evil thoughts molest
With this I shield my breast,
May Jesus Christ be praised.

The powers of darkness fear
When this sweet chant they hear,
May Jesus Christ be praised.

The demons of Hell cannot stand Spirit-filled praise! That's why David cried, "I will bless the Lord at all times, His praise shall continually be in my mouth." He knew the power of praise, and therefore, simply obeyed God in this matter, whether he felt like praising Him or not. He *chose* to praise (a matter of the will) which is essential to spiritual, mental and physical victory. In fact, praise and obedience are the prerequisites to spiritual health and would be better regarded as "preventive medicine."

Great care should be given to the type of music used in worship and praise. Much of the so-called Christian music in our day does not cause demonic spirits to flee, but rather beckons them to come. The story was recently told of the American missionary who introduced some "contemporary" Christian music to the elders of an African church. As the record played, the elders cried, "Why do you bring us music that calls evil spirits?"

What a rebuke to the satanically mesmerized American church! These natives were obviously Spirit-filled men who therefore were sensitive to the spirit realm of Hell. Let us praise God with music and words which Scripturally and awesomely lift our souls toward Heaven beyond the sensuality of the flesh, the world and the Devil.

Repentance and praise, therefore, are God's remedy for sin and oppression. In addition, the believer needs to confess and forsake his sin, moving in the path of obedience. He may also need to make restitution with those he has offended because of his rebellion. Certainly Saul needed to get right not only with God, but with his family and nation whom he had led astray. No man sins to himself — he will eventually affect others.

Sometimes Satan will continue to slander us even after these steps have been taken. What then? James tells us to "submit to God, resist the devil and he will flee from you" (James 4:7). We shall discuss this principle of warfare in more detail in a succeeding chapter. Suffice to say here that when we are assured that God has forgiven us (I John 1:9), then we must declare our authority over Satan. It is right here where most believers fail because of ignorance or unbelief.

Let us launch out with God, keeping short accounts with Him before whom all things are "naked and opened." Obedience is the key to victory, for what God said, He means. "By faith . . . Noah . . . moved with fear" and built the ark. Here is an illustration of the fear of God in action. Do you believe God? If so, your faith will result in obedience to God's Word.[4] The following words by James Stammis challenges our faith:

When we walk with the Lord
In the light of His Word,
What a glory He sheds on our way!
While we do His good will,
He abides with us still,
And with all who will trust and obey.

Trust and obey,
For there's no other way,
To be happy in Jesus,
But to trust and obey.

[4]See Hebrews 11 where "by faith" every servant of God *did* something in obedience to his Lord. True faith *always* results in obedience to God's Word.

CHAPTER 7

How Does the Mind Affect the Body?

Thus far we have considered two basic facts concerning the believer and his mind. First, the saving grace of God produces a sound mind (salvation of the mind). Paul challenges a young, timid preacher named Timothy that the spirit of fear is not from God. Included in salvation is a healed mind, a mind that is right with God — "the mind of Christ."

Second, this same grace provides deliverance from satanic attacks on the mind. Being saved does not exempt one from depression or other enemy invasions into the mind; however, God has provided His Spirit and "whole armour" for the deliverance and sustaining victory of His children. But what about the effect of one's thinking process upon the body?

Repeatedly, we have been confronted with the Scriptural axiom "as a man thinketh in his heart, so is he." A man whose mind process is linked to a depraved heart will live a depraved life. In contrast, one who has the mind of Christ will demonstrate a godly life. What is resident within a man must eventually come out in one form or another. Poison in the mind will eventually create poison in the body.

In his helpful book *None of These Diseases,* Dr. S.I. McMillen makes the following observation:

> Peace does not come in capsules! This is regrettable because medical science recognizes that emotions such as fear, sorrow, envy, resentment and hatred are responsible for the majority of our sicknesses.

> Estimates vary from 60% to nearly 100%. Emotional stress can cause high blood pressure, toxic goiter, migraine headaches, arthritis, apoplexy, heart trouble, gastro-intestinal ulcers and other serious diseases too numerous to mention.[1]

Psychosomatic illnesses are mushrooming nationwide. Increasingly, doctors are faced with the ability of the mind (psyche) to produce varied disturbances of the body. Our hospitals are jammed with people who hurt in body, but the real problem is in their mind. As Dr. McMillen further states:

> Invisible emotional tension in the mind can produce striking visible changes in the body, changes that can become serious and fatal. This concept should give us a new perspective on conditions that are often contemptuously referred to as "being in the head." Obviously, such conditions as vomiting, diarrhea, asthma, diabetes and deformed arthritic joints are not "in the head," yet these and scores of other serious diseases are triggered by tension in the mind.[2]

The writer visited a lady in the hospital who, when asked concerning her problem exclaimed, "I have three ulcers, one for my husband and one for each of my two children who are all driving me mad!" Indeed, she was physically sick, but her key to permanent cure could only come by dealing with her inward malice.

Sugar pill prescriptions do wonders for the patient who just "thinks" he's getting well. This is a basis upon which Christian Science and other psychic innovations operate — it is mind over matter. These false systems have a high "healing" rate because they have utilized a true principle that the body is controlled by the mind. How ironic that demonic doctrine and practices have propounded healing while the church of God is all but silent in this area.

[1]S.I. McMillen, *None of These Diseases* (Westwood: Fleming H. Revell Company, 1963), p. 7.

[2]*Ibid.*, p. 60.

There are many people in the world suffering great pain because of mental sins. The Scripture has much to say about the effect of the soul (mind, emotions and will) upon the body. Job, for instance, contrasted the condition of two individuals in death. One dies "in his full strength, being wholly at ease and quiet . . . and his bones are moistened with marrow." The other dies "in the bitterness of his soul and never eateth with pleasure" (Job 21:23-25).

This passage is very revealing. Notice the clear parallel between the soul and body of each man. The former dies with an inner quietness or tranquility, his bones therefore being moistened rather than dry and brittle. The other dies with bitterness in his soul, and thus was prevented from enjoying his food and good health. The inference here is that the digestive juices and vital organs (including bones) are greatly affected by inward emotion or thought process. In this case, bitterness has taken its toll, for our physiology (body) is always influenced by our psychology (mind).

We know that our bone marrow manufactures red blood cells for the body. The bones are linked with the synovial membrane which produces a viscid fluid, lubricating the joints of our skeletal system. Bitterness — a sin of the mind, when prolonged can prevent these marvelous and vital functions of the bones. The result may be a red blood cell deficiency called anemia. The common and dreaded disease of arthritis is also a likely possibility. The bitter spirit may serve to dry up the lubricating fluid, causing inflammation of the joints. In fact, it might be interesting to investigate how many of those who suffer from arthritis have had extended periods of bitterness.

Solomon says that envy will do the same thing — produce "rottenness to the bones" (Proverbs 14:30); but "a sound heart" free from envy, is the "life of the flesh" (or health). Again, the bones can be dried by a "broken spirit" (melancholy, depression, etc.), but a "merry heart doeth good like a medicine" (Proverbs 17:22). This is an exhortation indeed on the utter necessity of "internal medicine."

The same writer exclaims from the positive stance that if we "fear the Lord and depart from evil, it shall be . . . marrow [literally 'moisture'] to [our] bones" (Proverbs 3:7-8). Make no mistake; one's relationship to God can make a vast difference in his health. This is not to say that all sinners are physically sick and all true saints are well; however, sickness can be used of God to encourage one to consider where he stands with the Lord Jesus Christ.

Not only are these afflictions prevalent in the world, but unfortunately they are all too frequently found among God's people. Years ago, A.B. Simpson wrote a pointed article challenging saints to manifest "sweetness of spirit":

> Spiritual conditions are inseparably connected with our physical life. The flow of the divine life currents may be interrupted by a little clot of blood; the vital current may leak out through a very trifling wound.
>
> If you want to keep the health of Christ, keep from all spiritual sores, from all heart wounds and irritations. One hour of fretting will wear out more vitality than a week of work and one minute of malignity or rankling jealousy or envy will hurt more than a drink of poison.
>
> We do not wonder that some people have poor health when we hear them talk for half an hour. They have enough dislikes, prejudices, doubts and fears to exhaust the strongest constitution. Beloved, if you would keep God's life and strength, keep out the things that kill it; keep it for Him and for His work and you will find enough and to spare.

The above article presents one reason why saints forfeit physical health: The self-infliction of the body due to inward sin and subsequent failure to repent. Again we must make clear that not all sick believers are sinning. As Watchman Nee says:

> In God's redemption, the handling of sickness is unlike that of sin. With the latter, its destruction is totally uncircumscribed; with the former, this is just not so. Timothy for instance, continued to have a weak stomach. The Lord permitted this weakness to remain with His servant. So

in God's salvation, sickness has not been eradicated as totally as has sin. Some maintain that the Lord Jesus deals solely with sin and not with illness too; others can see the scope of His treatment to be as broad and inclusive as His treatment of sin. Yet, the Scriptures manifestly indicate to us that the Lord Jesus deals with both sin and sickness; only His healing with sin is limitless while that with sickness is limited.[3]

This leads us to the second reason why believers get sick. It is an indirect result of God's chastening. Paul left Trophimus ill at Miletum (II Timothy 4:20) and recommended that Timothy use a little wine for his stomach ailment (I Timothy 5:23). The great apostle himself suffered with "a thorn in the flesh" (II Corinthians 12:7) which has been interpreted as everything from eye trouble to a demon. Whatever the case, these three men were firebrands for Christ, and yet, to our knowledge, were sick. None of them was healed. What can we say except that it was ordained for them to endure suffering as an integral part of their Kingdom training. Indeed, "whom the Lord loves He chastens."

In addition, it must be said that those who hold that the atonement of Christ nullifies sin and sickness to the same degree have a real problem. Granted that God has made provision for the redemption of the whole man (spirit, soul and body); yet, as has been previously stated, the soul and body are still being saved progressively. This accounts for the fact that we still have wicked thoughts, emotional "jags" and a will that makes wrong choices; for the same reason our bodies are still subject to disease.

Sin *was* completely dealt with at the cross; yet, sickness is dealt with in the present, at least, on a limited basis. The reason for this is the inescapable fact that sin does not produce holiness in believers, but sickness can and does. Sickness, though part of the curse, can be used by the chastening hand of God to promote godliness in the believer. Sin,

[3]Nee, *op. cit.,* 3:184.

on the other hand, can only produce further corruption. This is an essential difference which needs to be faced by modern "faith healers" who indiscriminately pronounce folks "healed" without ever knowing their spiritual condition or the will of God in the matter.

While some allow no place for sickness in the child of God and judge their spirituality thereby, there are those at the other extreme who allow no place for healing. Both of these positions are Scripturally erroneous. It is amazing how men are like a pendulum, oscillating from one extreme to the other.

There are those today advocating what may be called "speaking a word" or "confessing" things into existence. For instance, if you have a cold, you simply reject it by confessing that it doesn't exist (even though your eyes are watering and your nose is running). This borders on "Christian Science" or the self-deceiving rejection of reality. Yet, this position makes sense if you *think* sickness is never in the plan of God.

We must not belittle the above concept however, because far too many Christians tolerate illness that God desires to cure. Again, they *think* that all sickness is ordained of God to make them "more spiritual." This represents a fallacious understanding of God's Word. God has made provision in the church for divine healing according to James 5:14-16. While many have explained away this position of Scripture, the serious believer must weigh it prayerfully.

The Lord has ordained elders in the church who, among other things, are responsible for ministry to the sick.[4] The afflicted saint is "to call for the elders." Immediately, this suggests a step of faith on the believer's part. This faith also presupposes that he has dealt candidly with God about the matter. You see, the key factor in healing is right here — dealing with the root cause of the sickness before God. This cannot be stressed too strongly.

Confession of sin is vital in this context, for disobedience

[4]Elders were the primary spiritual leaders in the early church, not deacons. See qualifications of elders in I Timothy 3:1-7 and Titus 1:6-9. Note "elders" (plural) in the "church" (singular) indicating a plurality of leadership in each local church.

may be the cause of the illness. When the sin is dealt with, then God grants a release and the prayer of faith for healing can be ministered. Some interpret this passage to mean a saint who has been disciplined by the church. The admonition of "confess your faults" (literally "sins") one to another may justify this concept, for restitution with other believers in the local assembly may be a prerequisite to healing.

Overall, the prayer of faith must be the result of a clear channel of fellowship between the elders, the sick believer and God. The root causes must be honestly exposed and corrected, followed by a unified will-of-God witness in all concerned. The writer can testify of the Lord's miraculous healing grace when the Scriptural precepts are fulfilled.

God has promised to wholly sanctify His people "spirit, soul and body" (I Thessalonians 5:23). It follows therefore that His desire, generally speaking, is for His children to be healthy in every way. Again there are always exceptions, for some notoriously vile people have hardly been sick a day in their lives.

Conversely, some of the saintliest folks have hardly spent a day without pain. Yet, there is a fundamental principle of healing throughout Scripture and we must seriously consider God's balance of truth on this vital issue. Again, "as a man thinketh in his heart, so is he."

The Lord told Israel after they were redeemed from Egypt, that if they would "diligently hearken" to God's Word and "do that which is right in His sight," He would protect them from the diseases of Egypt (Exodus 15:26). He further reveals His intent through the revelation of His name (*Jehovah Rapha* — "I am the Lord that healeth thee").

It is obvious that God fulfilled that promise, for nowhere in the wilderness wanderings is there a reference to a medical doctor. The Lord kept them in health except when they rebelled. In Numbers 21, for instance, God plagued them with poisonous snakes (serpents) which took many lives. Moses was commanded of God to raise up a brass serpent on a pole before the people, and all who gazed upon it were healed. Notice that healing came by faith in God's divine intervention and not through a "snake-bite kit."

The "brazen serpent" is a type of the Lord Jesus who identified with the serpent's curse (Satan). He "took our infirmities and bore our sicknesses" (Matthew 8:17) and on the cross became God's divine object of healing. John beautifully portrays this event when he states: "As Moses lifted up the serpent in the wilderness even so must the Son of man be lifted up" (John 3:14). Yes, one need only to "look and live." Christ alone is the Great Physician for our total need (spiritually, physically, mentally, etc.).

For reasons already discussed, God does not heal everyone physically. Yet there are those who could be healed if they came to grips with the cause of their sickness. Why then are not more people in better physical health? Apart from the previously mentioned reasons of self-afflicted illness and God's chastening, there are at least four other reasons why Christians are ill.

First, God judges the sin of believers by means of sickness and infirmity. You remember, for example, that some of the early church believers were desecrating the Lord's Supper. They were using the occasion to excessively imbibe in wine and food. Paul exhorts them to examine themselves because, as he states, "for this cause many are weak and sickly among you and many sleep" (I Corinthians 11:30). What a horrible indictment upon those who profess godliness. Not only was there physical malady among them but some were even *dead* (remember King Saul?).

Nothing short of repentance and confession of sin could remedy this situation. So it is with individual believers and whole churches today. God may be dealing with His sick child about his waywardness and rebellion. He should, therefore, not be so eager to get well until he knows the cause of his illness. Self-love prompts people to run immediately to the doctor, never considering what God is saying. Not that calling a physician is wrong, but the Lord should be sought first.

Other members of the church frequently are not much help to a distressed brother who may be under the conviction of sin. Instead of considering this possibility, we glibly and indiscriminately pray, "God, heal Brother Smith, if it be thy will." How often we enter the hospital to pray for an afflicted brother in Christ, never discerning the real source of his problem.

The elders who are called to pray for a sick one must be sensitive to this issue if their prayer is to be truly one of faith. God uses sickness to get our attention when other means have failed. Let us therefore be good disciples and hearken to His personal ministry to us or His message to others through us. Sin must be dealt with before God — this is the key to mental, spiritual and physical health.

Second, there are many today who are sick primarily because they want it that way. Believe it or not, some folks are so in love with themselves that they thrive on the attention and sympathy of others. In their way of thinking, the best tactic to use for such attention is to stay "sick." Multitudes delight in conversing about their aches and pains along with their "surgery." Such people find life unbearable if they cannot be the center of attraction. They receive an almost sadistic pleasure by chronically peddling their tales of woe. Obviously, such a person has a sinful mental attitude that must be corrected by grace. Here is another example of how faulty thinking reaps destructive behavior.

A third motive, although likewise stemming from self love, is to be sick in order to escape personal responsibility. Their reasoning is this: "If I am sick, then I can stay in bed and nobody can reprimand me for not doing my job." In other words, if you can convince yourself mentally that you are ill, then you can "cop out" of your responsibility.

On visitation night or prayer meeting at church, for instance, Brother Smith all of a sudden doesn't feel well and stays home. This illustrates that our flesh takes the road of least resistance. We must rebuke ourselves and others who have been deceived by a lying mind.

How prevalent this technique is in the world, where folks are no longer drunkards but "alcoholics"; no longer sex perverts but "gays." Murderers are increasingly pleading "insanity" for the same reason. The rationale is simple, "if I can make my problem a sickness rather than a sin or a crime, then I'm not responsible for my actions." Again, the remedy is not to change the labels for sin and make them sickness; rather we must deal with sin forthrightly and honestly so as to foster Holy Spirit conviction which in turn leads to repentance (change of mind)! Here is where unbelieving doctors and counselors offer little help in producing permanent change. A true biblical counselor can, by means of God's Word, bring permanent help to such people.

Fourth, there are some believers who are not healed because of biblical ignorance. While we have demonstrated that it is not God's will to heal everyone, there are clear promises of healing in Scripture that should be considered. There is a balance in this teaching that is essential for our day. Jesus *did* come to heal those "oppressed of the devil" and to "bear our infirmities." An afflicted saint needs to know this, for he cannot appropriate that about which he is ignorant.

James said, "Ye have not because ye ask not." "Whatever ye shall ask in my name," Jesus said, "that will I do, that the Father may be glorified in the Son." The key here is knowing what we possess in Christ and then with an obedient and expectant heart to make our request known. Note that Scripture never promises answers to prayer for our selfish gain, but always that God might be glorified.

In closing, may I suggest some principles of approach to God for healing or deliverance in the midst of life's trials?

1. Regard every difficulty (e.g., sickness, trial, etc.) as a challenge from God; remember He has all things under His control.

2. Seek God as to the cause of your affliction; if sin is involved, confess it to the Lord.

3. Make sure that you are thoroughly right with God and others.
4. Approach God in faithful prayer, pleading His promises.
5. Expect a successful spiritual victory in that situation.
6. Don't tell a soul until the matter is successfully resolved; no premature testimonies.
7. When the anticipated answer comes, then glorify God and testify of His goodness.
8. If the expected answer should be delayed or aborted, then thank God for His providential, all-knowing work in light of Romans 8:28-29.
9. Do not question God or become bitter at the outcome. Remember, God is still God. You are not omniscient. If God doesn't deliver us immediately, He obviously has a higher purpose to work out in our lives.
10. Continue in obedient expectancy for the next opportunity of faith.

Just this final word to the unbeliever or unsaved reader going through great trauma. Please consider that God loves you and may through this trial, be getting your attention. He wants you to turn from your sin and believe on His Son Jesus Christ who alone can minister to you in body, soul and spirit. Believe Him now, for this is the day of salvation for *you!*

CHAPTER 8

Waging War on Worry

"What's on your mind?" This common cliche speaks a world of truth in light of all we have discussed thus far. Whatever *is* on our mind is that which dominates our lives at that time. Again, "as a man thinketh in his heart so is he." It is vitally imperative, therefore, to think right in order to live right. The "worry wart" will invariably suffer defeat on the basis of this principle.

Anxiety is reaching epidemic proportions in our country and is probably the leading factor in psychosomatic illness. It is probably one of the most popular sins in humanity, passing off as a very "natural" problem of life. Even Christians have for too long regarded worry and anxiety as normal behavior; after all, "everybody does it!"

What does the word actually mean? The closest biblical term is "careful" *(merimnao)* as in Philippians 4:6: "be careful for nothing. . . ." The root meaning *(merizo)* is "to draw in different directions or distract"; thus to have a distracting care or anxiety. Paul's command to "be careful for nothing" does not suggest carelessness, but rather to refrain from being troubled with cares or carrying unnecessary burdens. Jesus uses the word in Matthew 6:25, translated "take no thought"; again this does not support thoughtlessness but rather anxious or undue thought.

"Anxious" or "worry" do not occur in Scripture per se but certainly express the biblical word *merizo* mentioned above. The dictionary defines anxious as "trouble in the mind respecting some uncertain matter." "Apprehensive" and "fearful" would then be synonyms. Worry means to be "uneasy in the mind; to feel anxiety about something, to fret." In fact, the Anglo-Saxon root idea is to "strangle or choke" — a true description of its destructive force. Worry will "choke the life" of victory right out of us. Someone has aptly said, "You can't change the past, but you can ruin a perfectly good present by worrying over the future."

When the apostle exhorted Christians to stop worrying, he was personally aware of its destructive effects on one's life. Being caught in many difficult situations, his faith was severely tested. These perilous experiences are vividly enumerated in II Corinthians 11 where he relates the beatings, stoning, shipwreck, etc. Then he caps the list with this statement, "beside those things that are without that which cometh upon me daily, the care *(merizo* — 'anxiety') of all the churches" (verse 28).

In essence, he is saying, "as if the tremendous trials and persecutions weren't bad enough, I have to worry about the spiritual needs of all these churches." It seems if anyone had a right or excuse to worry, Paul did; yet under divine inspiration he forbids it, though he himself had bouts with anxiety.

We sing the song "Burdens Are Lifted at Calvary," and that includes the burden of worry. Conversely, God *gives* burdens at Calvary too; however, these are the right kind, like prayer, Bible study and a desire for souls. These might best be called concerns rather than burdens. Significantly, God wants us to bear His yoke; that is, to enter into the burdens that burden Him. Concern for others is vital, and with the Lord's enablement we can minister effectively. However, if we are weighed down with the cares of this life, then we are bearing the wrong kind of burdens. That becomes worry rather than concern.

Jesus deals with the subject at great length with His disciples. He knew what a paralyzing effect worry would have on their future ministry. By way of introduction He tells them that "no man can serve two masters, for either he will hate the one and love the other; or else he will hold to the one and despise the other. Ye cannot serve God and mammon [wealth]" (Matthew 6:24).

Jesus strikes the surface cause of worry — preoccupation with materialism prompted by fear regarding the supply of daily necessities. They were faced with the needs of life, as we are, and the temptation was to be mastered by material gain rather than by God. Of course the root cause of worry is the sin of unbelief before an all-sufficient God. Therefore, we are exhorted to "seek first the kingdom of God"; that is, to be mastered by the Lord and His divine plan and consequently witness His faithful hand in meeting daily needs.

By way of personal testimony, I can joyfully relate to God's faithfulness on the basis of Matthew 6:33, which says "seek ye first the kingdom of God and His righteousness and all these things shall be added unto you." This framed verse has been visible in our home for the past twenty years. God has reminded us repeatedly that when He is first in our lives, all other loves and needs fall automatically into proper perspective. How many were the times in college when food and money were depleted and God sent "an angel unaware" to meet our needs. In specific answer to prayer, based on this promise, God intervened with exact timing and quantity.

Worry only stifles the blessing of God in our lives. He delights to shower His children with "good things" as they line up with Him (Matthew 7:11). Remember, you can't be praying, obeying and worrying at the same time!

In light of the potential grip of anxiety upon the disciples, Jesus exhorts them to:

> Take no thought [*merizo* — worry] for your life [literal soul], what ye shall eat, what ye shall drink; nor yet for your body what ye shall put on. Is not the life [soul] more than meat [food] and the body than raiment [clothing]?

He tends to excite their faith by reiterating the principle that the life (soul or inner being) is more important than food and clothing. In other words, if their lives which God redeemed are in line with His will then the lesser needs will be met. We interfere with God's ordained plan for us when we worry.

With this, Jesus illustrates the Father's care over the birds, who know nothing about anxiety as they fulfill their Creator's purpose. There is a rebuke intended here, for if lesser creatures like birds can "trust" their Creator, how much more should a redeemed man trust his God.

The oft-quoted dialogue between two birds strikes both a comical and serious note in regard to worry:

Said the Robin to the Sparrow,
"I should really like to know
Why these anxious human beings
Rush around and worry so?"

Said the Sparrow to the Robin,
"Friend, I think that it must be
That they have no heavenly Father
Such as cares for you and me."

Not only is worry an evidence of unbelief but it is utterly senseless. Jesus asked His followers, "Which of you by taking thought (worry) can add one cubit unto his stature?"[1] Obviously, no one can add eighteen inches to his height by worrying about it.

How many today are worrying about their height, weight, popularity, bills, retirement, etc. only to find that things get worse instead of better. In fact, how many, including Christians, are popping pills and paying extravagant medical costs because of a twisted psychology. They *thought* that things would get better if they anxiously nursed them, only to discover that "the table turned" — the wrong way.

Little do we realize the devastating effect worry has on the Christian's life and testimony. The world demands

[1]"Stature" *(helikia)* is primarily used as an age or certain length of life (e.g., John 8:21, 23). It can be used, however, with individuals as referring to a time of life or height.

more of us because of our profession of faith in the omnipotent, immutable God. How many believers have literally gotten ulcers through worry, and thus testified to the world that they are "unbelieving believers."[2] If this stabs the reader's soul with guilt, then frankly it is time to declare war on this worry-monster! Take heart, for soon we shall discuss some steps to victory over anxiety.

Probably the most outstanding biblical example which speaks to the issue is that of Mary and Martha (Luke 10:38ff). Both of these sisters were believers and yet their minds were running on two different wavelengths. Martha had welcomed Jesus into her home and was basically engaged in getting things ready for the meal. Her labor of love is commendable, especially in our day when the art of hospitality has waned. There is nothing wrong with being a good housekeeper and host; however, Martha was "cumbered about with much serving." This means she was overly occupied (literally "distracted") with household things, and had thereby been sidetracked from her unique Guest.

Mary, her sister, was sitting at Jesus' feet intently absorbing the words of her Saviour. Martha, being provoked at Mary's seeming disinterest in setting the table, asked Jesus to make Mary move. Our Lord's response is monumental and gives a key to mental sanity in a "workaholic" age. He said:

> Martha, Martha, thou art careful *[merizo* — "worried") and troubled about many things. But one thing is needful: and Mary hath chosen that good part, which shall not be taken away from her (Luke 10:41-42).

The point of focus here is that Martha was bogged down or overly concerned about legitimate work details. Evidently she had failed to prepare her heart "at Jesus' feet" so as to perform her service to God's glory. Martha

[2]It is common knowledge that ulcers in the stomach, colon, etc., are psychosomatic in origin, basically from anxiety.

worked in the flesh when she could have moved in the Spirit. She got caught up in the work of the Lord, but somehow missed fellowship with the Lord of the work. How prevalent is this situation in the present-day church — pastors, teachers and missionaries not excluded. This can only lead to a "nervous breakdown."

Some may accuse Mary of being lazy or super-pious, sitting while Martha was serving. God has never condoned laziness or piety that negates hard work. Mary's commendation by Jesus suggests that she had already done her work prior to Christ's visit; or at least she was drinking in the Word of God in preparation for her chores later on. She had learned the art of meditation — a missing note in present-day Christendom.

These two ladies represent the entire body of Christ today — those who are enduring the work of the Lord and those who are enjoying His work. Which group are you in, dear reader? Remember much of what passes off for Christian service today is either motion or commotion, rather than devotion. We must have more "Marys" if the church is to powerfully influence the world and bring glory to our God.

Besides triggering ulcers, how does worry rob us? One precious spiritual commodity which anxiety steals is the peace of God. Every redeemed believer has "peace *with* God" by justifying grace (Romans 5:1), but very few saints have the "peace *of* God." Here is the intimate, abiding and relaxing tranquility of soul, emanating from the Divine Comforter. That's what Mary knew by faith and what Martha missed by worrying.

Worry will also stymie our growth in grace, paralyzing our ability to stretch out in ventures of faith. In turn it will hinder and limit our effectiveness as a servant of God, stealing our authority to proclaim victory over the world system.

True worship and praise are nullified by anxiety, for we are caught in the ruts of mistrust and fear. The joy of the

Lord which was our strength has likewise been pilfered by this diabolical nemesis. This can only lead to defeat, depression and disaster. Unfortunately, this is exactly what is happening to the modern-day church. Unless God mercifully intervenes, we shall witness in our generation an alarming increase of spiritual "shipwrecks" and suicides. The life and death of King Saul will no longer be considered so bizarre and unique.

But thanks be to God, Who promises that "when the enemy comes in like a flood, the Spirit of the Lord shall raise up a standard against him!" The present surge of biblical counseling across our country is part of that standard and offers great encouragement in offsetting the incompetence of secular "Christian" psychology. A new day is dawning, when suffering souls have a biblical alternative to the notorious psychiatric "treatments" which frequently lead to "legal" drug addiction and institutionalization.

The nouthetic or direct biblical confrontation approach to counseling espoused by Dr. Jay Adams and others, has had unparalleled acknowledgement and success in the last decade.[3] More recently, under the leadership of Dr. John Huffman, the Analytic Counseling field was providentially launched and given professional licensure status.[4] These two systems are identical in their unswerving allegiance to the Bible as God's answer to every dilemma of man.

Worry has left behind it a trail of devastation inside and outside the church. Is there any cure? That is if we take a direct biblical approach and see it as God does. For too long worry has been excused as "doing what comes naturally," rather than calling it what God does — sin! This is the first step to victory.

[3]See Dr. Adams' book *Competent to Counsel* for his basic philosophy and approach to counseling.

[4]Through Dr. Huffman's leadership, the Pneumiatric (healing of the spirit) profession gained licensure expression by the Oklahoma State Examining Board of Analytic Counselors. A license from this board is recognized by the American Association of Analytic Counselors.

When God says, "be anxious for nothing" that is what He means. To transgress this command is to sin against God, Who enables one to live supernaturally above the natural. His commands are always accompanied by divine enablement.

Like any other sin, anxiety must not be excused away as a "weakness" or "problem." Christ didn't die for "problems" but for sinners and their sins. The problems result from our depravity; thus if sin can be overcome by Christ, the result and problem can likewise be remedied in due time. There is a biblical solution to every problem within man even though sometimes the surrounding circumstance cannot be altered.[5]

When confronted biblically with the sin of worry, one may react in several ways. He may 1) deny it; 2) attempt to avoid the thoughts causing it; 3) rationalize it with "oh well, everybody does it"; 4) drug it with pills, alcohol, hyperactivity, etc., or 5) do it God's way — CONFESS IT!

Scripture states that "if we confess our sins, He [God] is faithful and just to forgive us our sins . . ." (I John 1:9). Sin must not be hidden, for "he that covereth his sins shall not prosper but whoso confesseth and forsaketh them shall have mercy" (Proverbs 28:13). The word confess literally means "to say the same thing" or to agree with another. In this case, God says:

"Tom, you've sinned through worry — that's plain distrust in an all-sufficient, loving God."

With that Tom replies:

"Yes, Lord, I *have* sinned through worry. I've certainly failed to trust You as my all-sufficient and loving Heavenly Father."

Notice that Tom doesn't dodge the issue by making an excuse like, "but Lord, I couldn't help it," etc. He forthrightly agrees with God about his sin and openly con-

[5]For example, a man may find God's forgiveness and spiritual liberty in a prison cell. While his heart's problem has been remedied, his outward circumstance may not change for some time.

fesses it — that is the initial step in curing the curse of worry.

Not only is the monster of worry to be confessed, but it must be conquered. Here is where the warfare really begins. Feelings of fear and anxiety do not automatically subside immediately after confession. Satan delights in slandering God's promises to us with lying darts like, "You're not forgiven"; "See, you still feel guilty — God hasn't answered your prayers." Right here we must "stir up the gift of God within us" and focus our minds upon the Word which assures our forgiveness through Jesus Christ.

We must now appropriate by faith the mind of Christ — that ability to see the circumstance through God's Word and the prevailing victory of Christ in our behalf. Faith, not feelings, must dictate to the situation. The Bible says I no longer have the spirit of fear, but power, love and a sound mind. I choose (will), therefore, to believe God and bring my mind under God's control; that is, every thought being brought captive "to the obedience of Christ" (II Corinthians 10:5). I obey God in my mind — that's the key to victory. I've submitted my entire being to God. Therefore any continued mental fear and slander need not be tolerated. James tells me at this point to "resist the devil and he *will flee* from you" (James 4:7).

Resisting Satan, however, insures only temporary release. We must throw every care (anxiety) upon God because He has a genuine concern for us (I Peter 5:7). Bringing our thoughts and cares under Christ's control must become a habit if we are to habitually overcome worry.[6] But how is this accomplished? There is a biblical way.

Having confessed and initially conquered anxiety, this spiritual stability can only be achieved as we continue in prayer communion with God. Listen to Paul's familiar exhortation to "be careful (anxious) for nothing; but in everything by prayer and supplication with thanksgiving

[6]A habit is an "automatic, repetitive response."

let your requests be made known unto God" (Philippians 4:6). What is the main thrust of this verse? Simply this: If we are to be anxious for *nothing* then we must pray about *everything.* True prayer is the expression of a faithful soul resting in the security of his Saviour. As someone aptly wrote:

Faith came singing into my room,
And other guests took flight;
Fear and anxiety, grief and gloom,
Sped out into the night.

I wondered that such peace could be;
But faith said gently,
"Don't you see,
They really cannot live with me."

The prayer that conquers worry is more than asking God for needs (that is supplication). Prayer here implies an active communion with God in worship and submissive devotion. It is requesting our needs as an overflow of a yielded and devoted life. This kind of prayer cannot co-exist with worry. Someone has written:

> Prayer is an acknowledgement of faith; worry is the denial of faith. Prayer is putting my hand in God's, trusting to His loving guidance; worry is withdrawing my hand and denying His power to lead me. Prayer leads through the door of faith into the presence of God; worry leads through the door of anxiety and into the darkness of loneliness and discouragement. If prayer rules the life, victory results.

What kind of victory? God says His peace "which passeth all understanding shall keep your hearts and minds through Christ Jesus" (Philippians 4:7). Glorious truth! God's peace (comfort, rest, wholeness) shall keep (literally, "garrison or protect as a military guard") our hearts (spirits) and minds (souls) in Christ Jesus. Thank God, there *is* a remedy for worry. "Thou wilt keep him in perfect peace whose mind is stayed [fixed] on thee;

because he trusteth in thee" (Isaiah 26:3).

To you fearful anxious souls who read these words and have never trusted in Christ — stop right here and receive Him now! "As many as received Him, to them gave He power to become the sons of God" (John 1:12). Let Him demonstrate His great love to you for whom Christ died, that you too might know the peace of God that surpasses all comprehension. Then rejoice with Barbara Ryberg who wrote:

He does not lead me year by year
nor even day by day,
But step by step my path unfolds,
my Lord directs my way.

Tomorrow's plans I do not know
I only know this minute;
But He will say, "This is the way
by faith now walk ye in it."

What need to worry then or fret,
the God who gave His Son
Holds all my moments in His hand,
and gives them one by one.

CHAPTER 9

The Power of Right Thinking

It cannot be said too frequently that a man's actions cannot rise above his thought life. Whatever captivates our minds will eventually control our deeds. Words are powerful enough, but thoughts are even more consequential because they affect man's entire organism.

It has been unmistakably demonstrated that the body is stimulated and controlled by the mind. Psychosomatic illness is running rampant in our society and the end is not yet in sight. The testimony is clear, "as a man thinketh in his heart so is he." Right thinking produces right action, while wrong thoughts yield wrong conduct. Like kind produces like kind. Every individual reproduces himself to some degree in others. It is imperative, therefore, that our thoughts line up with God. Is that possible?

Apart from a saving relationship to Jesus Christ one cannot think properly. The unregenerate mind is in rebellion against God Almighty. Paul, in his letter to the Colossian believers, states:

> And you that were sometime alienated [from God] and *enemies in your mind* by wicked works, yet now hath He reconciled (Colossians 1:21).

God sees the "wicked works" of the unsaved as resident within the mind. My dear unconverted friend, without a "right" (sound) mind, you can never please God and that right mind is found only in Christ Jesus the Lord. "Let this mind be in you which was also in Christ Jesus" — receive Him as your Lord and Saviour from sin. Bow before His cross, for here it is that true life begins. It *is* possible to line-up with the true and living God.

The primary consideration underlining a sound mentality is the utter necessity to know who God is. The power of right thinking is resident only in God Who made the mind. A faulty concept of God can only result in erroneous thought and life patterns. Therefore, it is essential to have an infallible revelation of God. What is that? Thank God, it is the Bible — the inerrant Touchstone for all faith and practice.

Apart from Holy Scripture, we don't know who God is. Men have attempted to conjure up mental images of God, which at best has only produced distorted representations of diety. The Word of God *alone* reveals the true God, Who can only be realized by the sinner through faith in Jesus Christ.

Scripturally speaking, only those in Christ are "normal." The sinner is abnormal because he is not reconciled to his Creator. Normalcy of mind can only be attained, therefore, by a heart-to-heart intimacy with the eternal God. Praise God, the normal spiritual life can be lived when one is rightly related to Jesus Christ. Thus the apostle exclaimed, "I can do all things through Christ which strengtheneth me" (Philippians 4:13).

With the proper concept of and relationship to God, the believer can live victoriously in the midst of any problem or conflict. Herein lies the foundational truth of this book. Having our minds saturated with God's Word, our hearts surging with His love, and our bodies surrendered to His will, we can courageously face *any* trial, demon or disaster — supported securely by a Sovereign God! Our Lord has given us "a sound mind" in Christ, from which stems healing to our whole being.

Man's basic problem therefore is not sociological or environmental — it is theological.[1] From various quarters

[1]Theology is the "study of God." Man's basic need is to be rightly related to his Creator.

comes the cry that people are victims of society and circumstance. Don't believe it! The great issue is a proper relationship between man and God (vertical), which results in a proper relationship to others (horizontal). The following diagram illustrates this truth.

Circumstances don't make men, but men make circumstances. Remember, Adam and Eve fell from God in the Garden of Eden — a perfect environment. Thus, by grace, it follows that the Christian can live for God in an imperfect environment — even in this wicked world.

Again, it must be emphasized that our inner being (soul and spirit) controls the outer (body). In other words, the body or tangible part of man is greatly influenced by the intangible part (soul and body). If we are to bring healing to the mind of individuals, then we must reach their intangible soul, of which the mind is a part (see Appendix A).

Modern psychiatry and psychology have attempted to reach man's mind (intangible) by "treating" the brain, which is part of the physical (tangible) body. While the brain computes, stores and organizes data, the mind alone can interpret and utilize that information.

To confuse the brain with the mind can only end in futility, for they are not the same. Freudian psychiatry has long regarded man as merely an organized clump of molecular protoplasm.[2] But man is more than molecules. He has a soul and spirit which cannot be touched or located, but there is no mistake as to its existence. To deny this fact is to miss the mark in any attempt to heal the minds of men.

Could this not be the reason that such frustration abounds in the psychiatric profession? To shoot the body full of drugs in an attempt to heal the mind is not only futile but idiotic. Our country is filled with millions of people who have been "treated" for mental illness and now walk around like drug-addicted zombies. Admittedly, their brains have been affected by the drugs, but there has been no healing of the mind. By comparison, the family physician who gives his patient a sugar pill for cancer might be a bit more "successful," even if only from a psychological standpoint.

Recently, this writer was confronted with a counselee who illustrates the futility of maltreatment. Over a course of four years, he had spent several thousand dollars for psychiatric care. The result? He became a legal drug addict, passively walking about like a zombie with the jitters. He was a Christian man who could not smile, and convinced (by himself and others) that he was an incurable "mental case."

The story doesn't end here, however, for today after three months of direct biblical counseling, this man is an active, joyous believer. He is off drugs, eating well, exercising and most of all, meditating upon and practicing the Word of God. For a time he "walked in the counsel of the ungodly," but now "his delight is in the law of the Lord" (Psalm 1:1-2). Through the power of right thinking and living, his whole being has been transformed.

What truth is conveyed here? Simply, that knowledge and

[2]According to the *Scientific Manifesto* (1850) major university scientists declared that all activities of living men can be explained by physics and chemistry. In other words, man is only a physical (tangible) being.

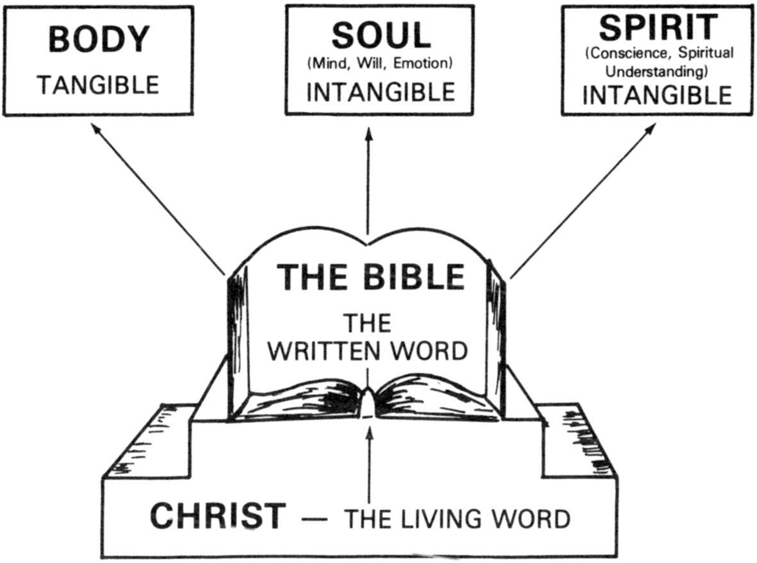

adherence to the Word of God is the basis of man's total healing. The Christian believer armed with Scripture not only can maintain a healthy mind himself, but can minister that help effectively to others. He can accomplish what no ungodly "professional" can.[3] Professional counselors, of whatever sort, are ultimately effective only as they adhere to and disseminate biblical principles.

In summarizing this section, the medical doctor basically treats the tangible (body) with the tangible (medicine, surgery, etc.). The psychiatrist treats the intangible (mind) with the tangible (drugs, shock treatments, etc.). But the Christian or biblical counselor treats the intangible (soul and spirit) and tangible (body) with the intangible (the Word, prayer, the Holy Spirit, etc.).

But how can the intangible Word reach tangible man? The answer is in Jesus Christ — the Eternal Living Word who became flesh (John 1:14).

[3]For further help and encouragement in counseling others, read *Competent to Counsel* by Jay Adams.

The Word of God (written and living) bridges the tangible (body) with the intangible (soul and spirit). Jesus said, "The words that I speak unto you, they are spirit and they are life" (John 6:63). God has ordained the Bible as His Manual for man's total mending and maintenance.

As a former pre-medical student, I appreciate the medical profession and recognize the legitimacy of its service. However, it is significant that in Israel's history the priest's function combined the physical and spiritual elements. There is no mention of a physician (see Leviticus 13). When Israel rebelled and thousands died of snake bites in the wilderness, God told Moses to hold up a brazen serpent on a pole. Those who gazed upon the serpent by faith were healed.[4] Here the spiritual and physical conditions were integrated. This connection must be seriously considered in present-day counseling. Again, "as a man thinketh in his heart so is he." Right thinking (on the Word) will produce the power to live right. But what about the "worry wart" who constantly frets over his circumstances. Is there any hope for such?

It was stated in the previous chapter that worry was sin and needed to be confessed to God — not tranquilized by pills. One should bring everything in prayer to the Lord, for worry and prayer cannot "live together" (Philippians 4:6). The problem, however, is that worry has become a common life-style leading to other deeper sins, and is not easily remedied. It is one thing to confess it before God; it is another thing to prevent its reoccurrence. What can we do?

The Scripture unequivocally teaches that sinful habits *can* be changed and *replaced* by godly ones. Listen to Paul's exhortation:

> Put off concerning the former conversation the old man which is corrupt according to the deceitful lusts; And be renewed in the spirit of your mind; And that ye put on the new man which after God is created in righteousness and

[4]See Numbers 21 and John 3:14 where the brazen serpent typifies Jesus Christ — The Sin-Bearer. This serpent on the pole significantly is the "trademark" for the medical profession.

> true holiness. Wherefore putting away lying, speak every man truth with his neighbor; for we are members one of another (Ephesians 4:22-25).

Offered here is no self-improvement course, or merely the "power of positive thinking." Rather, this means the "putting off" of my old life which was crucified with Christ (Galatians 2:20), and appropriating by faith ("putting on") the new life which I already possess in God. This is a divine-human transaction, whereby I take the resurrection power of Jesus Christ in exchange for my previously sinful practice (see Romans 6:1-14).

Therefore, if the mind is filled with worry, "put it off" (reject it) and take by faith the "mind of Christ." Appropriate the mental perspective and power of Christ given us by virtue of our position in Him. Is this not what Paul meant in Philippians 2:5 when he exhorted them to "let this mind be in you which was also in Christ Jesus . . . "? The context indicates their need for humility, which could be gained only by "putting off" pride and "putting on" the humility of Christ. This is possible to do because we already have the "mind of Christ" (I Corinthians 2:16). This is an illustration of possessing our possessions in God.

Unswerving conviction to God's truth is essential at this point. When the Word says we are "crucified with Christ," "dead to sin" (Romans 6:2), and "alive unto God" — take that as fact! In Christ, I need not be a servant of sin any longer. I *can* think right, and thus live right, because I *am* right with God.

This explains why the Word (Truth) must be hidden or programmed in our hearts if we are to live above sin (see Psalm 119:11). We have listened to Satan's lies for so long that we've embraced falsehood instead of truth. Moreover, we have been misguided by uncontrolled emotions which too often have dictated our behavior. Instead of exercising faith in the *facts* of God's Word, we have succumbed to our fleshly feelings, and sin has gained the victory. Let us keep telling ourselves the truth until we believe it. Away with the lies of Hell!

Faith is the spirit's sweet control,
From which assurance springs;
Faith is the pencil of the soul
That pictures heavenly things.

'Tis faith that purifies the heart;
'Tis faith that works by love;
That bids all sinful joys to part,
And lifts the thoughts above.

Faith is the victory that overcomes the world because it generates power to think Scripturally. Every person mentioned in the "Roll Call of Faith" (Hebrews 11) did right because they thought right, relative to God's Word. This is the key to spiritual triumph in any age.

The crowning need, therefore, is to have every lie in our minds replaced by truth. It is not enough to "put off" worry. We must "put on" or focus our minds upon the virtues of Christ. Herein is the crux of Paul's remedy for anxiety, expressed in Philippians 4:8:

> Finally brethren, whatsoever things are true, whatsoever things are honest, whatsoever things are just, whatsoever things are pure, whatsoever things are lovely, whatsoever things are of good report; if there be any virtue, and if there be any praise, *think* on these things.

Our polluted thought-life has rendered the church powerless. The Scripture challenges us to be "transformed by the renewing of our minds" (Romans 12:2); that is, our minds must stop being conformed (adapted) to the sin-soaked influences and satanic philosophy of the world. We must be mentally decontaminated and then constantly "fumigated" by God's heavenly fragrance — the Word.

Some time ago a news report from London said that when opening a new wing of a city hospital, her Majesty the Queen received at the door the traditional "tussy-mussy." The article explained that "tussy-mussy" was a stiff bouquet of strong herbs (rosemary, thyme, mint and lavender) bound together with a ribbon. In Medieval England, it was always carried by the royal hospital visitor. Being held in the royal hand, the royal nose was buried in it when threatened to be overcome by the stench that lingered in the hospital wards of that day.

The Apostle Paul's exhortation in Philippians 4:8 (cited above) could be expressed as the Christian's "tussy-mussy." Prayer by itself is not sufficient; our minds must be "buried" in God-honoring thoughts if we are to escape the stench of sin. Thus, Paul challenges us to "think"[5] or carefully reflect on certain things.

First, he says think of that which is *true.* Be preoccupied with facts, not falsehood. Christ is the Living Truth who has given us the written truth (the Word). Go to the infallible Source of truth — why settle for anything less? Here the believer finds the unfathomable depository for practical godliness and genuine service.

People speak of having the "real thing." The truth is *reality,* or that which lines up with the facts. Satan's world system is based on lies and is leading folks to disillusionment and destruction. God's kingdom is genuine "real estate," liberating those who know and practice the truth (John 8:32).

Second, we are to ponder those things that are *honest.* The word here pertains to that which is venerable or held in honor. We are to focus on that which is worthy of respect in a society that seems enamored with low, degrading things. For example, studies show that the average pre-schooler spends more than sixty percent of his waking time watching television. By the time the child is 14 he has seen 18,000 people killed on television. By the time he is through high school he has seen 350,000 commercials, many of which are not worthy of honor and tend to

[5]"Think" in Philippians 4:8 is *logizomai* — "to reckon or take account of." This is the word in I Corinthians 13:5 defining love as "thinking no evil" i.e., love doesn't reckon up or calculatingly consider the evil done to it! So we are to carefully calculate God-glorifying thoughts.

insult one's moral intelligence. The average adult now spends 10 years of his life before the "one-eyed monster." That's an incredible amount of time out of a short lifespan to indulge in flippant fun and games!

Add to this the barrage of sensuous music, cheap novels and idle chatter in which many indulge. How dare we who are dead to sin and are alive unto God continue to debauch and degrade our minds with such garbage? Certainly there are some noble things to watch and read apart from the Word. Let us be selective and get serious about honoring God with our minds (Matthew 22:37).

Third, we are exhorted to set our thoughts on things that are *just.* This refers to things that are right, conforming to the principles of God. We live in a day when people mock those who desire to "square" with truth and walk a "straight line." Ours is a lawless society, doing what is right in its own eyes. The results are devastating; look at the broken homes, prisons, mental hospitals, schools, etc., for a commentary on the "wages of sin."

Believer, though tempted to compromise with this drifting age, take your stand for the right, regardless of the cost. Remember, it is always right to do and think right. Let us dare to demonstrate in daily life the practical righteousness resulting from our saving relationship with Christ. By the Spirit's power may we focus our thoughts and actions upon God, "for the Word of the Lord is right" (Psalm 33:4).

Fourth, the Christian is to reflect on those things that are *pure.* This word denotes something uncontaminated or undefiled. The root is *hagios* from which we get "holy," "saint" and "sanctification." Here is a mind "set apart" unto God as an instrument to project only pure thoughts. What a challenge to any believer who lives in the midst of this crooked, perverted generation.

Premarital and extramarital sex, homosexuality, lewdness in music, magazines and television are taking their toll on society. This avalanche of filth has not failed to infiltrate the church. Many believers are battling for mental and spiritual survival because of yielding to impure thoughts — failing to "set their affections [mind] on things above, not on things on the earth" (Colossians 3:2).

Great shame has plagued the church through tragic entanglements of the saints with impurity. Spiritual adultery abounds because we have lost our "first love" for Jesus Christ (Revelation 2:4). James calls such "adulterers and adulteresses," in love with the world. Our Lord calls us to repentance (change of mind) and reconciliation to our unblemished Redeemer. Purity *or* impurity of the mind will unquestionably influence our loved ones because our thoughts are projected through attitudes and words. Is your mind pure?

Fifth, we are to think on those things that are *lovely.* The word literally means "toward-love," and only used here in the New Testament. "Lovely" is that which is acceptable or pleasing. Some translate it "lovable." To clutter our minds with the violence, sadism, occultism, vulgarity, etc., erupting from today's media is anything but "lovely."

The concept of agreement and unity with others is resident in this word. Thoughts of strife, bitterness and jealousy toward others can only rob our peace of mind. Let us deal with such sinful thoughts and "endeavor to keep the unity of the Spirit in the bond of peace" (Ephesians 4:3). "Behold how good and pleasant it is for brethren to dwell together in unity" (Psalm 133:1).

Sixth, do our thoughts center on things of *good report?* The literal rendering is "well-saying," or that which builds good reputation and speaks well of another. Be careful what you listen to. Many believers who may not have a problem with impurity are instead malicious gossipers. Watch it! Let us not engage in character assassination nor listen to those who thrive on "putting down" people.

We are commanded to restore (not tear) our fallen brethren with a "spirit of meekness" (Galatians 6:1). Furthermore, we must build up one another in our walk with God. Each of us needs all the help we can get in these critical days. Is it a good report? If not, reject the thought, and most of all, don't say anything.

Paul summarizes his list of right thinking qualities by challenging believers to reflect on things virtuous and praiseworthy. Virtue has the idea of moral excellence — the inner quality that rises above the worldly and mundane pitfalls of life. Peter uses it in reference to the excellence of our Lord Jesus Christ whose virtue (majestic splendor) is to be manifested through God's children (I Peter 2:9). What thought could be more virtuous than that of our peerless, precious Saviour. He is the object of a powerful, virtuous mind.

One final consideration is the matter of thoughts that are praiseworthy. This has nothing to do with self praise but rather that frame of mind which has God's praise or approval. Are we conscious of focusing on those things which glorify our Father in Heaven? Certainly all these virtues: truth, honesty, justice, purity, loveliness, and good report find their culmination in the person of Jesus Christ. He indeed is the Helmet of Salvation which we must "put on" if we are to experience victory in our thought life.

The power of right thinking is simply the ability to replace wrong thoughts with right ones. But the reader may comment, "Yes, that does sound good, but I still have all kinds of mental battles. How can this kind of thinking become reality to me? In the next chapter, the writer shall attempt to describe some practical strategies and resources to effectively engage in spiritual warfare.

If the reader, however, has not been savingly converted to Christ, right thinking is utterly impossible. These godly virtues can only be manifested in one's life by the presence and power of the Holy Spirit. My friend, stop here and seek God; repent and receive Jesus Christ as your personal Lord and Saviour. Do it now!

CHAPTER 10

A Strategy for Mental Warfare

A friend said to me one time, "I've sung 'Onward Christian Soldiers' for fifteen years before finding out that I was in a warfare." How tragic that so few believers, including Christian leaders, really come to grips with the true spiritual conflict. After expounding the believer's lofty position in Christ, Paul relates the reality of satanic struggle which shall inevitably result.

> Finally my brethren, be strong in the Lord, and in the power of His might. Put on the whole armour of God, that ye may be able to stand against the wiles of the devil. For we wrestle not against flesh and blood, but against principalities, against powers, against the rulers of the darkness of this world, against spiritual wickedness in high places (Ephesians 6:10-12).

Dear Christian, notice that "resting" in Christ will lead to "wrestling" with the forces of Hell. The cheap gospel of our day has made Christianity a "sunny, funny excursion" from earth to glory. God says we are in a battle that began in Heaven before man ever came on the scene.[1] Although Jesus Christ was manifested to destroy the works of the Devil (I John 3:8), the saints must wage war against the adversary from the victory gained at the cross.

Many believers are defeated because of ignorance in the spiritual realm. Due to insufficient teaching or disobedience (or both), they have operated in the fleshly realm but know little of the spiritual. We have walked by sight

[1]See Revelation 12:7-9, "war in heaven"; also Lucifer's fall in Isaiah 14:12f; Ezekiel 28:11f.

and feeling for so long that a walk of faith is considered strange indeed.

In connection with warfare, Paul commands that the Christian "be filled with the Holy Spirit" (Ephesians 5:18). A supernatural battle takes supernatural power. The early disciples were taught the Scriptures by our Lord after Calvary; but their consciousness of the real existence of the spiritual realm came following Pentecost. The Holy Spirit's filling (Acts 2:4) marked the real starting point of their spiritual warfare. That same Peter, who previously succumbed to the defeat of denial, now filled with power, boldly assaults the bastion of unbelief and thousands are converted!

Dear saint of God, if Jesus Christ and the disciples needed to be filled with the Holy Spirit (Matthew 3:16; Acts 2:4), how dare we presume to serve God without that enduement of power? How can we experience the joy of a sound, healthy mind unless our entire being is mastered by Jesus Christ? Herein lies the great need of the church today.

The promise of God's fulness is part of every believer's birthright in Jesus Christ (Acts 2:38-39). Let us lay claim to our "possession," for without it we have no basis of strategy in spiritual or mental warfare. Make no mistake; Satan is playing for keeps. We must get serious and enter the fray, prepared and empowered by the Holy Spirit.[2]

A warning is in order. Don't confuse the filling of the Spirit with some mystical, once-for-all victory syndrome. We are not talking about visions, dreams, flashing red lights, etc. — we are speaking of "fighting the good fight of faith." There is no passivity (floating of the mind) here, but an active, aggressive attack against the world, the flesh and the Devil, being prayerfully fought from our heavenly position of rest in Christ.

Passivity of mind is a great deceptive strategy of Satan.

[2]Those interested in further study on the Holy Spirit's fullness should consider the book *Heaven's Throne Gift* by Dr. James A. Stewart (see the back cover for additional information).

Confusion abounds in the world today with the Holy Spirit and wicked spirits vying for the minds of men. Occultism is mushrooming simultaneously with the experiential surge of the "Charismatic renewal." Advocates of both profess visions, revelations and other phenomenal manifestations. The true believer must beware of any doctrine that suggests "letting go" or losing control of our mental processes. Satan is a counterfeiter, and a passive mind becomes his playground in which to perform his deceitful tricks.

The Christian is to exercise his mind, and the Holy Spirit's fulness will enable him to do just that. We are *not* demonstrating spirituality when we permit our minds to go "blank" and wait for some feeling or outside force to move us. Yes, our spirit and will must be submissive to God and His Word; however, He delights and demands that we think His thoughts, as we have explained in the previous chapter.

Certainly, God wants to destroy our fleshly works, but never our personality. He does not desire that His people be devoid of thoughts, emotions, decisions, etc. Rather, He invites us to think and feel what He thinks and feels. The enemy takes advantage of us when we are unable to exercise our spirit and mind.

I remember visiting a Christian man who had dropped out of church quite suddenly. Having been previously active in the ministry, he was seated in the living room gazing into space. Upon inquiry of his welfare, he pompously informed me that he hadn't read the Scriptures nor prayed for weeks. "And I don't care either," he said. "God is the only one that can do these things and He hasn't moved me."

This dear man was waiting for God to do for him what was really his responsibility. No doubt that when his supper was ready, he did not sit on his hands and say, "Lord, feed me," but picked up his knife and fork and "dug in." Why not be as practical in gaining spiritual nourishment?

Here is an example of a lopsided theology and resultant passivity by which Satan gained a victory.

Great care must be taken not to lose sight of the biblical balance between God's sovereignty and our responsibility. We are to "work out our salvation" (cultivate, obey the Word, etc), because God is "working in" us to perform His will (Philippians 2:12-13). We are working *out* what God is working *in.* The Holy Spirit does not bypass man's personality, but rather moves people themselves to work. An evil spirit demands inactivity in a man so he (the spirit) can work in his place, reducing the man's soul to a robot.

Herein is an important distinction between the work of the Holy Spirit and that of an evil spirit. Beware of passivity of the mind — keep it actively focused and renewed on the Word. More shall be said in this vein in our next chapter, where we consider Scriptural meditation. Remember the Holy Spirit's anointing, along with Scriptural obedience, serve as a base for every strategy in the believer's arsenal.

If inner healing is to be perfected, then the mind must not only be changed (repentance) and Scripturally activated, but *controlled.* Martin Luther once said regarding thoughts, "You can't prevent the birds from flying over your head but you can keep them from making a nest in your hair." It is not the coming of thoughts that present the problem but rather our invitation to have them settle down in our minds. We are bombarded by wicked ideas from the world, the powers of darkness and our own depraved hearts. To harbor these thoughts will only bear the fruit of sinful action. Even disturbing thoughts, when allowed to remain, will "rattle" our lives. Thoughts must be controlled!

But what if a Christian has already lost control of his thought life? Sin has surfaced and he now suffers from defeat, guilt and discouragement. Thank God, there is divine strategy based on Christ's sacrificial death, called confession of sin (I John 1:9) and repentance (Revelation

2:5). It is imperative that the offender come out of hiding and deal honestly with his sin. The promise is "he that covereth his sins shall not prosper, but whoso *confesseth* and *forsaketh* them shall have mercy" (Proverbs 28:13).

This mercy and forgiveness need only be claimed by faith, for as someone has said, "Forgiveness is a fixed fact." Remember, beloved, that in Christ, "We have redemption through His blood, *even the forgiveness of sins*" (Colossians 1:14). This means "*all* trespasses" (Colossians 2:13) — past, present and future! Our God is full of grace and the believer's sins have been dealt with once and for all. "It is finished," cried our Saviour from the cross. The debt of our sin was "paid in full":

My sin — oh the bliss of this glorious thought —
My sin, not in part, but the whole,
Is nailed to the cross and I bear it no more;
Praise the Lord, Praise the Lord, O my soul!

Right here we need to consider a problem situation that is creating mental horror in myriads of saints. I speak of the relentless mental harassment of sinful thoughts having just been confessed to God. We have believed God for His forgiving grace and cleansing power, but lo, we have no assurance of forgiveness. Instead, we still feel guilty and someone whispers, "You're not forgiven," or "God forgave you the last time but now — you've gone too far." The guilt now swells into horror and the feeling of hopelessness hurts the soul.

What's happening? Has God abandoned us and His promises? No, a thousand times NO! We have just witnessed a choice strategy of Hell called a "guilt trip." This is not from God, but a demonic attack not only on our minds but against the veracity of God's Word and character. Here is a repeat performance of the Serpent's "hath-God-said" slander to Eve in the Garden (Genesis 3:1). What strategy can we use to deal with such an attack?

May I say first, by personal testimony, that this form of

satanic conspiracy almost drove me to suicide, until God graciously showed me the Scriptural remedy. The burden of this book is a result of the devastating bouts with demonic accusations and the glorious healing that God ministered to my mind.

I had only been in the pastoral ministry two years when one day an anxious fear gripped my soul. I cried out to God for deliverance, but to no avail. In this instance, it was not a matter of forgiveness, but the principle is the same. God knows, I wanted to obey and serve him explicitly. I didn't know it then, but Satan cleverly slandered my desire to obey God by suggesting that I "make up" with the enemies that I had made through preaching the Gospel.[3]

I hadn't done anything wrong in this case, and I certainly wanted to obey God. I loved these enemies, but they sure didn't love me. My first attempt ended in disaster and the fear and guilt feelings paralyzed me. I could not pray, read the Word or preach. For two solid weeks I walked around as a "mental case," while my dear wife faithfully and tenderly ministered to me the best she could. I thought this was of God, yet every move I made to "obey" only heightened my fear.

I left town for a few days to get away from the situation, but the situation followed me. Finally, in desperation, I fell at my bedside and cried out to God for hours. I was finished — washed up — ready to take my life, if I could not have God's peace. Then at once, my tearstained eyes fell on these words, "For God hath not given us the spirit of fear; but of power, and of love, and of a sound mind" (II Timothy 1:7). The truth of this Scripture shot through my fatigued mind like a streak of lightning!

God had used this verse on another occasion, but now it came through with renewed power. I realized then that

[3]This attack was subtle because we should attempt to be reconciled to our brethren (Matthew 18:15f); but these folks were enemies of the cross with whom there had never been any fellowship.

Satan, not God, was "commanding me," and the fear, likewise, was satanic and not godly. The deceiver had "pulled a fast one" on me as he did with the first couple in the Garden.

Jesse Penn-Lewis comments on this method of deception as "working upon an innocent creature's highest and purest desire, and cloaking his own purpose of ruin under the guise of seeking to lead a human being nearer to God."[4] Oh, the release that came when I stood firmly on the Word of God and resisted the Devil's attack! I was then able to face my enemies with fear-conquering love when the occasion arose. God was in control, not Satan. What a joy to be led "beside the still waters" in the "presence of mine enemies."

Since then I have practiced what I call the "red flag" strategy. When *any* kind of fear or guilt strikes my mind, a "red flag" goes up (mentally). I know now, from experience, that this is Satan's choice approach, at least to me. Therefore, I verbally confess my submission to God; then on the authority of the Word (James 4:7), I *verbally* resist Satan and expect him "to flee."

The Apostle John reveals the conflict of the ages between God and the arch-accuser of the brethren.

> And there was war in heaven: Michael and his angels fought against the dragon; and the dragon fought and his angels, and prevailed not; neither was their place found anymore in heaven. And the great dragon was cast out, that old serpent, called the devil, and Satan, which deceiveth the whole world: he was cast out into the earth, and his angels were cast out with him. And I heard a loud voice saying in heaven, Now is come salvation, and strength, and the kingdom of our God, and the power of his Christ: for the accuser of our brethren is cast down, which accused them before our God day and night. And they overcame him by the blood of the Lamb, and by the word of their testimony; and they loved not their lives unto the death (Revelation 12:7-11).

[4]Jesse Penn-Lewis, *War on the Saints* (Nashville: The Lighthouse, n.d.), p. 3.

According to this passage, our ancient foe has already been conquered by our Lord Jesus Christ. On the basis of that victory, the saints "overcame him by the blood of the Lamb" and by the word of their testimony to Satan to make him cower and flee! Hallelujah!

Jesus foretold Satan's opposition to the church when He said to Peter:

> Simon, Simon, behold, Satan has desired [literally "begged"] to have you, that he may sift you as wheat; but I have prayed for thee, that thy faith fail not; and when thou art converted strengthen thy brethren (Luke 22:31-32).

Notice that the enemy's attack is no different today than in Peter's time. He is "begging" to sift out and destroy God's servants. But, thank God, our Lord's strategy has not changed either. On the basis of His finished work on Calvary, Christ is continually interceding for us in Heaven through the power of an endless life (Hebrews 7:24-25).

Our Mediator prayed for Peter, saving him to the "uttermost" (completely and forever). The same promise is for present-day believers. But note carefully that while Jesus interceded for Peter, He prayed specifically that Peter's *faith* would not fail. There is no allowance here for passivity in Peter's life. He must activate his faith if he is to overcome. Though held by God's omnipotent hand, yet he must exercise his God-given authority against the enemy!

What then is faith? Scripture itself defines it as "the substance [or substantiation] of things hoped for, the evidence of things not seen" (Hebrews 11:1). The evidence of biblical faith seems to be authority.[5] In other words, faith is the believer's authority to take God's authority on the basis of His Word.

Note that Jesus told Peter that when he was "converted" (turned around in victory) to "strengthen thy brethren" (Luke 22:32). Significantly, the apostle carries

[5]For instance, Moses at the Red Sea and Joshua at Jericho, etc.

out that command beautifully as recorded in the fifth chapter of his first epistle. Appealing to the elders to have "a ready [active] mind" (verse 2) and a humble spirit, he exhorts them to "be sober, be vigilant, because your adversary the devil as a roaring lion walketh about seeking whom he may devour; whom *resist* steadfast in the *faith*" (I Peter 5:8-9). How well Peter knew what he was saying!

Note that it is by standing firm in the faith (authority of the Word) that we conquer Satan. Jesus destroyed his works at the cross but, nevertheless, the believer must personally hold high the "shield of faith wherewith he shall quench *all* the fiery darts (missiles) of the wicked one." For "this is the victory that overcomes the world, even our faith" (Ephesians 6:16; I John 5:4). Peter strengthened his brethren after he found out, by experience, the indispensability of faith. So must we, in this evil day, launch this "red flag" strategy.

Dear believer, have you been slandered in your obedience, or has God's Word been maligned in your mind by the accuser of the brethren? Have you been cheated from the joy of God's forgiveness because the lion convincingly accused you of committing the "unpardonable sin"? Then put up your "red flag" — resist the devil and believe the truth of God's forgiving grace!

I sinned. And straightway, post-haste Satan flew
Before the presence of the Most High God,
And made a railing accusation there.
He said, 'Tis true that he has named Thy name,
But I demand his death, for Thou has said,
"The soul that sinneth, it shall die." Shall not
Thy sentence be fulfilled? Is justice dead?
Send now this wretched sinner to his doom.
What other thing can righteous ruler do?
And thus he did accuse me day and night,
And every word he spoke, O God, was true!
Then quickly one rose up from God's right hand,
Before whose glory angels veiled their eyes,
He spoke, "Each jot and tittle of the law

Must be fulfilled; the guilty sinner dies!"
But wait — suppose his guilt were all transferred
To Me and that I paid his penalty!
Behold My hands, My side, My feet! One day
I was made sin for him, and died that he
Might be presented faultless at thy throne!
And Satan flew away. Full well he knew
That he could not prevail against such love,
For every word my dear Lord spoke was true.

— Author Unknown

Agree with God when you've sinned in thought and/or deed, but also agree with God when He promises forgiveness. Remember, the Holy Spirit prompts or leads us to repentance, but Satan *drives* us to unholy fear. When satanic fears come, do not be passive, but boldly yield your authority in Christ, for He's "praying that your faith will not fail" — and it won't. Don't permit the "lion of Hell" to chew you up when the Lion of Judah has already knocked out his teeth! "Greater is He that is within you than he that is in the world."

The main issue to be faced here is the utter necessity to control our thoughts. Prevention and maintenance is much more advantageous than cure. Peter speaks of "girding up" the loins of our minds (I Peter 1:13). This figure of speech originates with the Eastern custom of dress. Men wore long, flowing garments and when desiring to run or work, they would "gird up their loins"; that is, they would gather up the loose ends and secure them about the waist with a belt.

So the believer must gather up the "loose ends" of his thought life and prepare his mind for action. If we don't, our enemy will search for the loose ends and tug them for all he is worth. Don't give him *any* strings to pull. Refuse to let your thoughts wander to and fro, but rather saturate them with God's truth.

Probably ninety-nine percent of God's dear children are abysmally ignorant or disobedient in this vital area.

Somehow, we have settled down in "grace" and switched our minds to "automatic pilot." My friend, that is nothing short of spiritual suicide. No wonder so few believers manifest any semblance of true victory in their daily walk.

> The passivity of the mind is due to a misconception of the meaning of consecration and obedience to the Holy Spirit. Many take for granted that the thoughts in their heads hinder their spiritual walk. They do not perceive that it is a brain that ceases to function or which functions chaotically that hinders spiritual life, whereas one which functions properly is not only profitable but also essential. Such a mind as this can alone cooperate with God.[6]

Paul commands us to bring "into captivity *every thought* to the obedience of Christ" (II Corinthians 10:5). A lying or lustful thought is an enemy of the soul and must be denied a place in our mind. How? By simply speaking the word: "I reject that thought and choose to keep my mind captive to Christ!" This is done on the authority of our sound mind in Christ (II Timothy 1:7).

The apostle also speaks here of "casting down imaginations and every high thing that exalteth itself against the knowledge of God." This involves thoughts that seem rational and innocent but smack of sinister pride. How clever is our foe to suggest, for instance, that we are "more spiritual" than our brother and need to get him "straightened out." This thought is vile, exalting itself against the Word and must be cast down by an act of the will.

Our hearts are "deceitful above all things and desperately wicked." Apart from mind control under the filling of God's Word and Spirit, the enemy will "ride" our corrupted thoughts for all he's worth. If he can't puff us up with proud thoughts, he will attempt to discourage us to death. Don't permit these thoughts to find lodging in your soul or they may well become mental ruts requiring radical

[6]Nee, *op. cit.,* III:23.

spiritual treatment. Consider the admonition of a sign post on a lonely country road, "Take heed which rut you choose. You will be in it for the next 25 miles."

Notice how God places the responsibility on the believer to think and live right. Imperatives like "cast down," "gird up," "meditate," "put-off," "put-on," etc., are addressed to the saints. God will not do for us what He has given us the ability to perform. This truth is absolutely indispensable to Christian victory. Fail here and you will fail indeed.

Redeeming grace has, among other things, freed our will to make right Scriptural choices. Here is the strategy that few believers understand. The soul is comprised of mind, emotion and will (see Appendix A). Depravity has taken its toll on each part, not the least of which is a perverted imbalance. Most people, including believers, are governed not by the will but by the emotions (feelings). When we greet folks, we never say "How do you will today?" Invariably it's "How do you *feel?*"

Repeatedly God instructs us to walk according to His Word — not by feelings, but by faith. This faith affects the will, which is man's God-given organ for decision-making. Man's will today is smothered by sickly, sentimental feelings which change (and change him) almost with the direction of the wind. Likewise, believers interpret their spiritual victory (or lack of it) on the basis of emotional highs or lows. This may explain why there are so many "yo-yo" Christians, constantly going up and down.

When the Scripture is clear and we know the decision pleases God, let us choose (will) to do right, regardless of feelings. When it comes to reading God's Word or going to work or church, and I don't feel like it — I *choose* to do it. When I know it's time to get up and my body refuses, I tell that body, "You move or else I'll drag you out of bed!" That is the way to treat our thoughts and actions — choose the right and consciously reject the wrong. Don't be passive and spineless. Exercise your will, regardless of feelings, and do right simply because it's right to do right.

We must briefly consider one final area of strategy and that is the healing of the memory. Many believers are in desperate need of divine surgery to remove from the mind the memory of tragic experiences. What a crippling effect the past has on precious souls. Multitudes are infected with thoughts and feelings of bitterness toward God and others. Resentment abounds because of ill treatment and unfairness.

Often someone will say, "I can forgive but I can't forget." Oh, my beloved friend, you *can* forget those things that are behind you and begin "reaching out" for God's perfect will before you. There is healing of the memory in Christ's provision, but again you must choose it. Paul says, "This *one* thing I do." He exercised his will in grace, determined to forget past failures, sins and ill-treatment. He knew God's healing of the memory which enabled him to go on in the high calling of God. So can you my friend. How?

First, face squarely any bitterness, etc., in your life as sin against God. Second, confess and forsake it (I John 1:9). Third, ponder the fact that an all-powerful and loving God permitted these past events as part of an overall plan to glorify Himself and edify you (Romans 8:28-29). Fourth, permit God to apply His healing grace to your mind and count it done.

Finally, refuse to ever discuss the problem with anyone or have anything to do with it again. When tempted to rehearse these thoughts, reject them immediately. Remember the "red flag" strategy? Trust God, for in Him you have salvation of the mind.

If you've been reading this, dear friend, and have been convinced of your lost, sinful condition, then turn to Jesus Christ right now while you still have breath. Bow your heart before Him and believe upon Him — choose Him *now!* The Bible says, "As many as received Him to them gave He power to become the sons of God" (John 1:12).

In summary, the believer in Christ has a spiritual arsenal totally adequate to maintain the healing of his mind. He is in warfare, to be sure, but the anointing power of God's Spirit, prayer and the Word has insured victory. Now he must and can control his life by choosing to do the will of God as revealed in Scripture. In Christ we have all the resources to fight and win the battle for our minds!

CHAPTER 11

Wanted: Scriptural Brainwashing

What is wrong with brainwashing? Nothing, if you use the right kind of "wash." Every human being is brainwashed to some degree by one philosophy or another. Depravity itself holds the creature captive to a satanically-inspired humanism, in direct opposition to God's truth. The natural unregenerate man "receives not the things of the Spirit of God . . . neither can he know them . . ." (I Corinthians 2:14). This is why a man *must* be "born again" (from on high) so his mind might begin to be deprogrammed from lies and programmed or "brainwashed" with truth.

For sure, the Communists are brainwashed. But so are the cultists, politicians, athletes and educators. Don't misunderstand, by brainwashing I do not mean the common definition, which is "the systematic alteration of personal convictions, beliefs, habits and attitudes by means of intensive, coercive indoctrination." And yet, there is a sense in which *everybody's* beliefs, habits and attitudes are influenced by some form of "indoctrination" (voluntarily or involuntarily). In whatever station of life, a person operates according to his doctrine (teaching).

The time has come for the church to seriously consider the need to be "indoctrinated" in the Word of Truth, for "sound doctrine" cannot be endured in our day (II Timothy 4:3). Men of God must concentrate on "preaching the Word" — the whole counsel of God (Acts 20:27), regardless of the present trend. A mighty brainwashing of truth is essential if the saints are to meet the challenge of effectively evangelizing this godless society.

As we have considered, the mind must be changed (repentance), actively renewed, and controlled. In addition, our minds must be occupied or indoctrinated. In this area, Communism is wiser than the church. For too long we have piously "sailed along" in spiritual passivity content with saying "I'm saved," while the world laughs at our lack of serious commitment. Mental and spiritual laziness abounds and the lackluster of the average Christian indicates that his mind is far from "delighting in the law of the Lord."

Many today have joined the health food and diet fad, rightly concerned about what enters and occupies their bodies. How few, however, have any real concern for what enters and fills their minds. As a poor diet affects our physical condition, so the health of the mind will be intensely influenced by our spiritual appetites. If we take in "garbage," we can only expect garbage to come out. What a man sows, that he reaps (and then some). This is a fundamental principle applicable even to our mental diet. We become what we think.

No believer can ever be successful before God apart from the meditation and observance of the Word. In light of the present-day emphasis on "how to be successful," only one mention of "success" occurs in Scripture. The Lord told Joshua:

> This book of the law shall not depart out of thy mouth; but thou shalt meditate therein day and night, that thou mayest observe to do according to all that is written therein: for then thou shalt make thy way prosperous, and then thou shalt have good success.
>
> Have not I commanded thee? Be strong and of a good courage; be not afraid, neither be thou dismayed: for the Lord thy God is with thee whithersoever thou goest (Joshua 1:8-9).

Every Christian would like to be a strong, courageous overcomer in this life. Yet, how few real soldiers of the cross grace the church today. The reason? God's spiritual fitness program has been sadly ignored. Everything has its price, and spiritual "sanity" is no exception.

Several factors have made it difficult for contemporary saints to engage in regular meditation and fellowship with God. First, there is the hectic, high-speed pace of modern society which counters the attempt to slow down and think. We're too busy to "wait on the Lord" — there's no time for quiet reflection. This generation of Christians has become so busy "doing" that we've forgotten how "to be." Some of us are so engrossed in the work of the Lord that we've lost touch with the Lord of the work. No wonder there are so many neurotic, exhausted saints. Beware of the barrenness of busyness.

A second factor nonconducive to meditation is the desire among believers for "instant" blessing. We must have success *now* or never. The fast-food craze has taken its toll in the church — "get it quick and eat it quick!" Instant coffee, tea, potatoes, etc., have given way more recently to an "instant Bible," for those who must get spiritual food *fast.*

Books like *100 Snappy Sermon Starters for the Busy Pastor* have great appeal to preachers desiring "instant" sermons. God's blessing and power through the Word takes time and effort. Any shortcut will prove to be abortive. Even in the Space Age, it still takes nine months for a baby to be born. Some things just can't be rushed.

Still another consideration stifling meditation is the seeming inability of people to be alone without desiring some kind of audible stimulation (radio, television, stereo, etc.). The art of quietude is all but lost, with "noise," not stillness, clamoring for our attention. Vance Havner refers to the "good 'ole days" when folks would stroll leisurely down a country road musing on the handiwork of God's creation.

Nowadays, he says, if someone walks down a road, people think he's either "lost or participating in an organized hike." Oh, for a return to the state of mental tranquility where God has opportunity to whisper His truth to our hearts. This is possible only by a conscious willingness and discipline to focus our attention upon the Lord.

Take time to be holy,
The world rushes on;
Spend much time in secret,
With Jesus alone.

In spite of the hectic, high-accelerated pace of life and the corresponding decline of Scriptural contemplation, mind-bending and meditative activity is on the increase. For instance, Transcendental Meditation is sweeping the country, especially in colleges and universities. Approximately 30,000 new converts a month are flocking to the TM Movement which claims remarkable benefits for body and mind.

There is one problem — TM is a satanic counterfeit for true biblical meditation. Yet, the world has enough sense to realize the great benefits of inner reflection, while the church continues in its religious "fun and games."

Advocates of TM usually sit with eyes closed, uttering a mixture of syllables known as "mantra."[1] Giving complete attention to their mantra, they shut out the rest of the world for fifteen or twenty minutes at a session, twice a day. Great results of mental, physical and emotional well-being are propounded among TM disciples. Yet, the movement is replete with occultic and demonic activity. One group claims the ability to fly or levitate, propelling their body outwardly by nothing but mind power.

The Spirit-filled believer immediately recognizes the anti-biblical character of TM, for our minds must only be captivated with the truth and power of God. Yet, if such remarkable results are claimed through these satanically inspired activities (i.e., TM, occultism, etc.), *how much*

[1] "Mantra" are the names of Hindu gods. Transcendental Meditation is an offshoot of the Hindu religion and is therefore *not* an innocent "non-religious" exercise.

more could be accomplished through God-ordained, Scriptural meditation?

Some perceive meditation as a mental "cop-out" or state of blankness. People talk of lying on the beach meditating on the cloud formations, while others are mesmerized by the television screen. This and similar activities (along with TM) are misguided perversions of biblical meditation. As stressed so vehemently in preceding chapters, the mind must never become passive or an open target for wicked thoughts. Our "mantra" must never be anything but truth or that which conforms to God's Word.

What then is true meditation? The Hebrew word *hagah* means to "moan, groan, utter or muse." There is no mental inactivity or passivity here. Biblical meditation is concentrating on one thought of God exclusively and consistently. This demands a deliberate act of the believer's will, for our flesh is naturally opposed to such activity. Thus the Psalmist said: *"I will* meditate in thy precepts . . . *I will* delight myself in thy statutes . . ." (Psalm 119:15-16).

The word "muse" has the idea of pondering or considering a thought at length. Satan's desire is to *a*muse[2] us or divert our thinking away from God. How much activity today passing off for Christianity is only amusement, and nullifies serious musing upon the things of God. However, if the enemy cannot divert our thinking to frivolity, then he masterfully leads us to muse on negative things (e.g., our weaknesses, failures, trials, etc.), which results in discouragement. We must *choose* to think right!

Another biblical concept of meditation is that of eating. Jeremiah states: "Thy words were found and I did eat them; and thy word was unto me the joy and rejoicing of mine heart . . ." (Jeremiah 15:16). Strength and spiritual nourishment are derived from meditating or "eating" the Word. "Desire the sincere milk of the word," said Peter, "that ye may grow thereby."

[2] "Amusement" comes from this word and is the opposite of meditation.

One of the choicest passages on the subject is the First Psalm where David describes the "happy" (blessed) man who "delights" in God's Word. To "delight" here is to take pleasure in, or give excited attention to, the Manna of life. This pictures one who has rejected the perverted counsel (food) of the ungodly and now eagerly devours the delicacies of truth (Psalm 1:2). By meditation, he has permitted "the words of Christ to dwell in him richly in all wisdom . . ." (Colossians 3:16). Jesus said: "Blessed are they which do hunger . . . after righteousness, for they shall be filled" (Matthew 5:6). Are you hungry for God?

Scripture must be the source of our meditation that we might maintain intimate fellowship with God. Food, however, must not only be taken into the mouth, but chewed, digested and assimilated into our entire being. Vitality and power to the body become reality only when the food is totally absorbed into our system. So it is with the Word of God. Yes, the truth must be read daily, but that is like placing food in the mouth and refusing to chew it. A certain amount of nutrient may trickle down the throat, but it will never satisfy the energy demand.

For one reason or another, most Christians probably never get to this first stage of nourishment (i.e., reading the Word), and then wonder why they have such a short supply of spiritual stamina. God doesn't feed us "intravenously"; *we* must take the responsibility of placing the food in our mouths. Let us choose to get into the Word, that the Word may begin to get into us.

A second essential step in eating is chewing food. The contents in the mouth are masticated and broken down in size and texture to facilitate digestion. Spiritually, this describes memorization of the Scripture — breaking it down so as to focus upon its life-giving energy. We must store up the truth in our minds that we may appropriate its strength when necessity calls. When confronted with a difficult situation at work, for example, the believer need not worry (negative meditation), but draw upon a verse from his memory bank, like "I can do all things through Christ which strengtheneth me" (Philippians 4:13). As he "chews" on the truth, life-giving encouragement begins to flow through his being.

But you say, "I can't memorize." That's ridiculous! Whatever excuse you may offer is only an excuse. One has said that "very dull minds become keen by holding them right down to the grindstone." The keys to memorization are interest and repetition.[3] You remember your name, address, telephone number, place of employment, etc. Why? Because you are personally interested in those things and use them repeatedly.

So it must be with God's Word. Take a verse (e.g., Philippians 4:13) and write it on a small card. Carry it with you all day, reading it over repeatedly at break time, lunch, etc. Learn a phrase at a time until it is stored away in the memory. Then review it frequently. Begin today!

The third essential stage of eating is digestion. By chewing and swallowing, the food reaches the stomach awaiting a further processing. Here the gastric juices attack the nutrients and a churning movement begins. Eventually, what originally entered the mouth will be assimilated, for the most part, into the bloodstream. Hence, energy will flow to every part of the body so as to facilitate work. This describes the function of biblical meditation.

As chewing and swallowing are insufficient to total digestion, so reading and memorizing the Word are insufficient for total mental soundness. Truth cannot simply live in the "stomach," it must be processed into the heart (spirit). Here is where the groaning, moaning and musing effect of meditation comes into play.

The mind now begins to focus and concentrate on some aspect of the Word. There is the "churning," restful labor that analyzes and absorbs every possible nutrient from the truth. Andrew Murray depicts meditation as: "Holding the

[3]Is it not amazing how many TV commercials children and adults remember without any conscious memorization? What could be done if we really determine to discipline our minds for God!

Word in the heart until it affects every phase of life." To be sure, some live to eat, but *we* must eat to live. Our concentrated analysis of Scripture must always lead to godly action, for this is the primary purpose of "food."

A lesson can be learned from the cow chewing its cud. A cow has various compartments in its stomach, likened to the diversity of the human mind. Food is swallowed into the first stomach where it is softened and molded into small masses called "cuds." Being then belched back into the mouth, the cud is chewed thoroughly and passed along to the "second" stomach to be eventually digested. From there it is transformed into milk, eventually bringing its rich nourishment to the consumers.

So the believer must "chew the cud" of God's Word if the "milk" is to be manufactured for consumption. We cannot effectively bless others with the Word until it has filtered into every compartment of our lives. Ponder it, utter it, groan over it, chew on it, then apply it personally; most of all, *obey* it to the glory of God, for this is the ultimate purpose of biblical meditation and spiritual success.

What results from biblical meditation? Listen carefully, for the fruit of godly exercise is incredible. David, in Psalm 1, likens the godly meditator to a "tree planted by the rivers of water, that bringeth forth his fruit in his season. . . ." Trees are prominent in stature, pointing upward toward their Source. So the believer is *prominent* in this world. He can stand up tall (upright) as God's redeemed "tree" — no longer bent over by the power of sin.

In fact, our standing in Christ is on "high" or heavenly places from whence comes the ability to keep our feet firmly fixed on planet earth. We are *somebody* in Christ — a "peculiar people," (i.e., His prize possession). He has called us to demonstrate His grace in a wicked world. Biblical meditation and obedience will make this calling a reality.

The meditating saint is a tree not only prominent, but

planted (Psalm 1:3). The word here literally means to be "transplanted." We were rooted down in Satan's kingdom originally (John 8:44), but God has "delivered us from the power of darkness and hath translated [transplanted?] us into the kingdom of His dear Son" (Colossians 1:13). We are not growing wild, but we are firmly fixed and rooted in God.

Roots insure stability when the winds blow. Palm trees are well-footed enough to withstand hurricanes. So the Word-saturated saint can stand in any storm of life because he's "rooted and grounded in God's love" (Ephesians 3:17). No need for mental breakdown or neurosis for the firmly planted Christian.

Another characteristic of trees is their *power* or indestructibility. Moses constructed the Old Testament Tabernacle with wood taken from the acacia tree in Palestine. These trees are famous for their defiance against the forces of deterioration. Likewise in Brazil, the quebracho tree is notorious for dulling the woodman's ax. So the child of God, indwelt and empowered by the Holy Spirit, is indestructible.

Walking in the will of God, nothing can destroy him. Paul was virtually immortal until God's purposes for him were fulfilled. Though stoned and left for dead (Acts 14:19), he was raised up to "finish the course" which God had ordained (II Timothy 4:7). As we've already emphasized, even Satan can't destroy us because "greater is He (Christ) that is in us. . . ." Martin Luther, in his phenomenal hymn "A Mighty Fortress Is Our God," describes the believer's indestructible authority in Christ.

And tho' this world with devils filled,
Should threaten to undo us;
We will not fear, for God hath willed
His truth to triumph through us.

The prince of darkness grim —
We tremble not for him,
His rage we can endure,
For lo! his doom is sure;
One little word shall fell him.

The trees of the Lord are also *prosperous.* In Christ, we are planted by "rivers of water . . . and whatsoever we do shall prosper." Picture a drought across the land, with blighting barrenness in every direction. But look! In the midst of it all stands a flourishing fruit tree exuding its fragrance and miraculously defying the arid conditions surrounding it. How well this portrays the Spirit-filled, meditating believer in the midst of the "waste howling desert" of the world!

Being firmly planted in Christ, the believer's root system constantly draws water from an unseen well . . . the Fountain of Life. "He that believeth on me," Jesus said, ". . . out of his belly [innermost being] shall flow rivers of living water" (John 7:38). There is no attack of the unholy alliance (i.e., world, flesh and the Devil) that need "wither" the supernatural prosperity of God's children. His "leaf" is ever-green as he abides in the Vine (Christ), apart from which he "can do nothing" (John 15:5).

By virtue of this continuous source of supply, the saint can enjoy the fruit of spiritual productivity. Those who "abide in me," Christ said, "the same bringeth forth much fruit" (John 15:5). The trees of the Lord have been "ordained" to produce fruit through the power of God's Word and Spirit (John 15:16). That fruit is the very character of the Lord Jesus Christ lived out in the believer by the indwelling Holy Spirit.

"Love, joy, peace, longsuffering, gentleness, goodness, faith, meekness and temperance" (Galatians 5:22-23), characterize the Spirit-filled meditator. This fruit is produced "in his season" (Psalm 1:3). When passing through a "season" of tragedy, the believer can experience the fruit of "peace." In seasons of doubt, there is faith; and in trying circumstances there comes longsuffering (patience), etc. Above all, the overwhelming supply of God's love wells up in every season.

Note that *every* child of God positionally has *all* he needs in Christ to live victoriously in this world (Ephesians 1:3). Practically, however, this spiritual prosperity can only be experienced consistently by those whose minds are occupied with the Word of God. Biblical meditation and obedience, therefore, are indispensable to abundant Christian living.

"If meditation is so vital to spiritual soundness," you say, "then just how do I begin?" That is a good question and deserves an answer. Briefly, let me suggest a course of action toward the goal of Scriptural meditation.[4]

1. *Make a definite commitment to obey God in this matter.* Determine that you *will* pay the price to have God's best. Remember, this is the key to mental and spiritual success (Joshua 1:8).

2. *Take time daily for meditation.* Set aside at least 15 minutes once a day for this purpose, preferably in the morning. Once you block out a daily time segment, don't let anything (e.g., radio, TV, telephone, laziness, etc.), interrupt or stop you.

3. *Arrange a definite place to meet God.* Total seclusion and quietness is essential to meditation. Consider this a divine appointment with God at a definite time and place. Don't break the date.

4. *Learn to relax in God's presence.* Most Christians are physically and emotionally tense. Stress and pressure attack us early in the day. We must therefore settle down with God beforehand in preparation for the warfare.

There is much talk today about "hanging loose." Bodily this is essential in meditation, while the mind is in "full gear." Meditation is primarily geared for the mind, not the body. As we relax, therefore, the mind is alert (not passive)

[4]The writer is indebted to Mr. James Johnson for these basic meditation steps as listed in his helpful book, *The Gift of a Sound Mind,* p. 42ff.

and ready to focus on God's Truth.

A technique known as "progressive muscle relaxation" can be used effectively to prepare your body for meditation. This procedure involves the rigid flexing or tightening of all body muscle groups, then permitting them to go limp or "hang loose."

For example, begin by tightening the muscles in your feet. Hold that tightly-flexed position for a few seconds and then "let go," letting the feet remain limp. Follow the same procedure progressively with your calf (lower leg) muscles; then the thighs, abdomen, chest, arms, shoulders, neck and face. With the body relaxed, you are now ready to exercise the mind.

5. *Select a verse or brief portion of Scripture.* Your choice should be determined by a particular need or desire in your life. For instance, if you've had difficulty with fear, you might take Isaiah 41:10 where God says, "Fear thou not, for I am with thee; be not dismayed for I am thy God. I will strengthen thee. . . ." Read the text repeatedly and begin memorizing the main thoughts. (See Appendix B for selected subjects and passages for meditation.)

Let God's truth dominate your mind as you concentrate upon it. "Chew" these thoughts one by one, digesting them to the point of saturation.

6. *Spend time in praise and adoration to God.* This is an opportunity to worship God, whose Word reflects His glorious Person and work. Meditate upon the greatness of God in His love, grace, creation, salvation in Christ (including a sound mind), etc. Then spend time praising Him for what He has done for you.

7. *End the session with prayer and application.* Through meditation the Holy Spirit will enable us to turn the Scripture into prayer and personal application. For example, Jesus said, "Follow me and I will make you fishers of men" (Matthew 4:19). Reflecting on that verse, you might pray for God's enablement to "follow Christ" as you go to work that day. In prayer, you claim the promise that He

will make you a "fisher of men" or soul-winner. Engaged in further prayer, you then set out to "fish" for men under the Spirit's leadership.

8. *Keep physically fit.* As the mind affects the body, so the body may influence the mind. Get periodic medical examinations. Hard work and exercise are still great sources of mental and physical therapy. Get proper rest. Maintain a balanced diet — lots of fresh fruits and vegetables, etc. Eat to live, don't live to eat! Consider the benefits of fasting, not only for weight loss and maintenance, but to sharpen the mind for greater meditative creativity.[5]

You have now meditated upon the Word of God which has inspired worship and praise to the God of the Word. Truth has now become personal, leading the meditator to prayer and practical obedience. Indeed, this is biblical meditation that redounds to the glory of the Lord and insures spiritual success (Joshua 1:8).

The mind must not only be changed, renewed and controlled, but *occupied.* The need is acute for Scriptural brainwashing among believers if the church is to valiantly "occupy" until Jesus comes.

With a biblically occupied mind, we *can* overcome every obstacle of life! Oh, for a reformation of Scriptural meditation in our day, that the church may powerfully demonstrate God's healing for the mind.

[5]For sound instruction on biblical fasting, see Johnson, *Ibid.*, chapters seven and eight.

Conclusion

The fight is still on! The minds of men are crumbling beneath the load of sin. Hospital wards are bursting with psychosomatics, while society in general has adopted a pill-popping mentality.

People seem incapable of solving their basic personal and family problems. Psychiatric and psychological techniques have offered little in permanent results due to an erroneous diagnosis of man's real problem and the resultant failure to apply the corresponding remedy.

Sin's depravity, not "mental illness," is the primary cause of the dilemma. Our problems are basically theological (God-related), not psychological (mind-related). Right thinking and conduct are possible only through a right standing with God by saving grace. The Word of God (the Bible), not the psychology textbook, has the therapeutic principles which reach *every* aspect of man's total welfare.

The fall of man took an awful toll on his spirit, soul and body. Originally created in God's image, his spiritual understanding of God, self, the world, etc., became distorted. His mind was now "sick," and in desperate need of healing.

The Lord Jesus Christ appeared in time to effectively and eternally destroy the sinner's sin. Healing came not only to the blind and deaf, but to an insane maniac. The healing ministry of Christ encompassed every facet of man's makeup — including his mind. Such saving grace is still available today for any who will embrace Jesus Christ by faith (John 1:12).

What about the need of those who are savingly joined to Christ and yet, suffer mental anguish? Many believers are gripped with paralyzing fear, rendering them powerless. Satan has been relentless in his intent to discourage and defeat God's people. We have learned, however, that God has not given us "the spirit of fear," but power, love and a "sound mind" (II Timothy 1:7). Perfect love casts out ungodly fear, and to fear the Lord is to conquer all other fears.

In addition, Satan takes every opportunity to harass the saints who give him place through their ignorance and unbelief. Mental depression and attacks of demonic oppression are prevalent even among the choice servants of God. We have seen this so clearly demonstrated in the life of King Saul. Yes, even suicide is not a stranger to believers who fail (for whatever reason) to obey God and activate their minds in appropriation of Christ's victory.

Does the mind, in any way, affect our bodily health? Indeed it does! How prevalent are ulcerated stomachs and dried up bones among Christians who have witnessed a deteriorated thought-life. Add to this the "cancer" of worry which has eaten away the spiritual and physical vitality of millions. This "killer" has virtually become one of the most popular and acceptable sins among the saints. It's time to declare war against this enemy of the soul!

Is there any help? Thank God, there is remedy in Jesus Christ, the Helmet of our Salvation. The curse of depravity has left our minds programmed with deception and falsehood (John 8:44). By regenerating grace, the believer now possesses the "mind of Christ" which makes Scriptural thinking a reality. Lies are being deprogrammed and truth is now reprogrammed into our hearts (Psalm 119:11).

We have discussed the power resident in right thinking. Wrong concepts must be replaced by clear, biblical principles. Scriptural meditation is indispensable to a healthy mind. Accompanied by obedience, this holy "brainwashing'' is guaranteed to bring success (Joshua 1:8).

Essential, however, is an understanding of and activation of the strategies for spiritual warfare. Protected by the whole armour of God, the believer must take the offensive against the host of Hell. With the Word, faith and Spirit-filled prayer, we can be vict*ors* instead of vict*ims*!

Having a mind that is changed, renewed and occupied with truth, we can be conquerors in *every* circumstance of life (Romans 8:37). Satan, sin and self are now subservient to the Spirit and Scripture-filled saint! Hallelujah! As we exercise our God-given authority and privileges, mental sanity will not only be our portion, but will eventually ''infect'' multitudes around us who desperately need healing for the mind. May God grant us a holy ''epidemic'' of mental salvation in this midnight hour of history.

Church of God, let us arise and meet the challenge of our day, occupying until He comes!

On every hand the foe we find,
Drawn up in dread array;
Let tents of ease be left behind,
And onward to the fray.

Salvation's helmet on each head,
With truth all girt about,
The earth shall tremble 'neath our tread,
And echo with our shout!

Understanding Man's Makeup

To better understand the mind, it is necessary to carefully consider man's creation and purpose in this world. We know from Scripture that man was made in the image of God (Genesis 1:27). He was ordained to reflect the character of the triune God on the earth. As God's unique creation, Adam was commissioned to reign over every living thing (Genesis 1:28). What a privilege indeed!

Being a reflection of God, man was constituted with three functions[1] — all geared to be a collective unit of praise to the Creator. Genesis 2:7 states, "The Lord God formed man of the dust of the ground and breathed into his nostrils the breath of life, and man became a living soul." At a glance, this would liken man's creation to that of animals, seeing that both have a soul function *(nephesh)*.[2] But a closer look at the Hebrew construction shows that man not only has a body and soul but a spirit which animals do not possess. Remember, man is a *human being* created in God's image — not an animal! We must make a complete break with the evolutionary hypothesis which would cloud our thinking in reference to man's true identity and position.

The Scripture states that "God breathed into man the breath of life and man *became* a living soul." "Breath" here

[1]This is commonly called the trichotomy view, i.e., men comprised of body, soul and spirit. Others believe men to be a dichotomy, i.e., body and soul.

[2]See Genesis 1:20 ("life") and verses 21, 24 ("living creature") are translated from *nephesh* (soul). This demonstrates that animals have a limited soul function (will, emotion, etc.). They do not, however, possess man's ability to reason or visualize concepts.

is not the common Hebrew word *ruach,* translated "breath" or "wind." Rather, the word here is *neshamah* which indicates a unique function in man. Nowhere in Scripture is this word or function attributed specifically to animals.

It is necessary here to search the Scripture carefully, not just to be technical, but to understand something of the grandeur and wonder of this creation called "man." If we know what God gave him in creation, then we can project man's potential for total effectiveness and success in Christ. Thus, let's consider the functions of this "breath of life" which sets man apart from every other earthly creature.

First of all, Job 33:4 states that "the Spirit of God hath made me and the breath of the Almighty hath given me life." The word "breath" here is *neshamah* as in Genesis 2:7. Notice that it gives "life" unto man. This is not to be confused with God's eternal life, but rather that principal of human life.[3] In fact, the phrase "breath of life" can be rendered "the breath *which is* life."[4] By this "breath," man became a "living soul." Watchman Nee comments that:

> As soon as the breath of life which became man's spirit came into contact with man's body, the soul was produced. Hence, the soul is the combination of man's body and spirit. . . . The soul is the meeting-point of spirit and body, for there they are merged. . . .
>
> The spirit cannot act directly upon the body. It needs a medium, and that medium is the soul produced by the touching of the spirit with the body. The soul therefore stands between the spirit and the body binding these two together. The spirit can subdue the body through . . . the soul, so that it will obey God; likewise the body through the soul can draw the spirit into loving the

[3]*Chaiyim* — a plural of abstract indicating the qualities and spiritual components of man's life. See *Gesenius' Hebrew Grammer,* Section 124d. This "life" is not divine, but *human,* since God's life was to come through partaking of the "tree of life" (Genesis 2:9).

[4]Genitive of Apposition — like "the city of New York," i.e., the city *which is* New York. See *Gesenius* — Section 127h.

world.[5]

The writer is aware that this quotation may sound strange and even confusing to those who have pictured man as having only a body and soul. Mr. Nee uses "soul" here in reference to the total man rather than the common usage as man's immaterial part. Many times in Scripture, man is referred to as a soul. For instance, in Genesis 12:5, Abram took Sarai, Lot and "the souls they had gotten in Haran" and went to Canaan. It is said of Jacob that "all the souls" (people) that came with him into Egypt totalled sixty-six (Genesis 46:26). Therefore, when Christ died for "souls," He died to save man in his totality.

Secondly, when God breathed this "breath" *(neshamah)* into man, He not only gave Adam human life, but a conscience as well. Proverbs 20:27 says that "The spirit *[neshamah]* of man is the candle of the Lord, searching all the inward parts of the belly." Note how the word for "breath" in Genesis 2:7 is here translated "spirit." This is definitely not God's Spirit, but man's God-given, human spirit. This spirit functions as the penetrating searchlight of God in the inner depth of man's being. Just as the candlestick in the Jewish temple searched out the dark corners, so God's "candle" within these temples (I Corinthians 6:19) searches and judges our motives. Though the word "conscience" is never used in the Old Testament, its function within man is obvious from this and other verses.

The third function of God's "breath" in man is spiritual understanding. Job 32:8 states that "There is a spirit in man and the inspiration *[neshamah]* of the Almighty giveth them understanding." God placed in Adam the ability to understand spiritual things. This is not to be confused with the "mind," which is part of the soul and possesses natural, intellectual and reasoning power. We are dealing here with man's ability to understand God as opposed to natural comprehension.

[5]Nee, op. cit. 1:23, 26.

Man may have a tremendous mind and yet be uanble to grasp the things of God. The Scripture says "they are foolishness to him" (I Corinthians 2:14). On the other hand, a person having minimal mental capacity may through newness of life in Jesus Christ possess tremendous understanding of God's Word. A converted child with simplicity of faith has a clearer spiritual insight of Scripture than an unconverted college professor. The issue is one of spiritual knowledge versus mere academic learning. It is a matter of quality rather than quantity of knowledge. Indeed, God's thoughts are not man's! Only the Holy Spirit can reveal the truth to fallen humanity.

This function of *neshamah* (or spirit) is equivalent to *nous* in the New Testament — translated "mind" (fifteen times) and "understanding" (seven times). For instance, in Luke 24:45, it states of Jesus Christ that He opened "their understanding, that they [disciples] might understand the Scriptures." This illuminating work of Jesus was obviously beyond the realm of mere intellect or mind capacity. Likewise, David prayed, "Open thou mine eyes that I may behold wondrous things out of thy law" (Psalm 119:18). It is obvious that he was not referring to his physical but rather his spiritual eyesight or understanding. How critical is the need for such understanding in the church today.

Thus, the primary functions of man's life-giving spirit are both conscience and spiritual understanding. This is man's vehicle of communication and fellowship with God (John 4:23). While this is a fascinating study in itself, we need to consider another part of man's make-up; namely, his soul.

The body is the material part of man divinely formed from the dust, while the immaterial parts (spirit and soul) were the result of divine inbreathing (Genesis 2:7). While it is impossible to dogmatically locate these immaterial parts or distinctions, the Bible does recognize the existence of each. Paul, for instance, prayed that the Thessalonians would be preserved blameless by God in their "spirit, soul and body'' (I Thessalonians 5:23). Again, the divine ministry of the Word is said to be ''sharper than any two-edged sword, piercing even to the dividing asunder of *soul* and *spirit* . . .'' (Hebrews 4:12). God makes a distinction between the function of soul and spirit, which greatly enhances our understanding of man's inner being.

In contrast to man's spirit which enables him to communicate with God, he possesses a soul or self-consciousness. This is the seat of our personality — the elements which make us human. The body and spirit seem to be merged in the soul (Genesis 2:7) to form our personality. This is why the Bible sometimes calls man ''soul'' as though this is all that he possesses (see Genesis 12:5; 46:27). Scripture indicates that there are three main faculties which constitute man's personality or soul: will, emotion and mind.

There are many verses to support these three aspects of the soul.[6] First, the volitional aspect of the soul is illustrated when David cried to the Lord, ''Deliver me not over unto the will [literal *nephesh* — ''soul''] of mine enemies'' (Psalm 27:12). This godly king also exhorts to ''set your heart and your soul to seek the Lord . . .'' (I Chronicles 22:19). To Solomon, he said, ''Know the God of thy father, and serve him . . . with a willing mind [literal ''soul''] (I Chronicles 28:9). It is clear from these examples that our soul is capable of making decisions and choices. Without this capacity to express our willingness, man would be reduced to a robot.

Second, the soul functions as a faculty of *emotion.* Everyone ''emotes'' to one degree or another and over one thing or another. This aspect of the soul is demonstrated beautifully in the relationship of Jonathan and David. The Word says that ''the soul of Jonathan was knit with the soul of David, and Jonathan loved him as his own soul'' (I Samuel 18:1). We see here the soul's capacity to love. That same soul, however, can feel grief (I Samuel 30:6),

[6]Nee, op. cit., 1:36-38. There are other aspects of the soul's function, but Mr. Nee cites the above as the three primary ones.

discouragement (Psalm 42:5), delight (Isaiah 55:2), sorrow (Matthew 26:38), and joy (Psalm 35:9). These and other feelings are necessary functions of the soul without which man would be rendered insensitive.

A third aspect of the soul, and that upon which this book focuses, is the *mind* or intellect. Man, unlike animals, not only has the capacity of God-consciousness *(nous)* but the ability to reason. His mind in conjunction with his brain becomes the instrument for thought and reflection. While the brain computes, stores and organizes data, the mind interprets and utilizes that information.

Consider Proverbs 19:2 which states "the soul without knowledge is not good." Again, hear David's exaltation: "Marvelous are thy works and that my soul knoweth right well" (Psalm 139:14). Most familiarly, however, is Proverbs 23:7 which teaches that "as a man thinketh in his heart [literally "soul"] so is he." The soul definitely has the capacity to think, thus functioning as mind.

It is significant that biblical language scholars recognize a great parallelism between the Hebrew and Greek terms *nephesh* and *psuchē*.[7] The former, we have recognized, as the Hebrew word for "soul." The Greek word *psuchē* is translated "soul" fifty-eight times in the New Testament. Our English terms psychology, psychiatry and psychosomatic are derivatives of this word, and all deal with the mind.

Note, therefore, the inseparable connection between one's mind and soul. To inquire as to the health of one's soul is to likewise be concerned for their mind's condition. The following diagram illustrates the God-given functions of man.

Needless to say, the complexities of man cannot be adequately understood or illustrated. The above aid is only an attempt to decipher three aspects of man's totality. Note that he has a God-given spirit comprised of conscience and spiritual understanding. This involves man's *God-consciousness* and could be likened to what the Scripture

[7]Ernest DeWitt Burton, *Spirit, Soul and Flesh* (Chicago: The University of Chicago Press, 1918), p. 73.

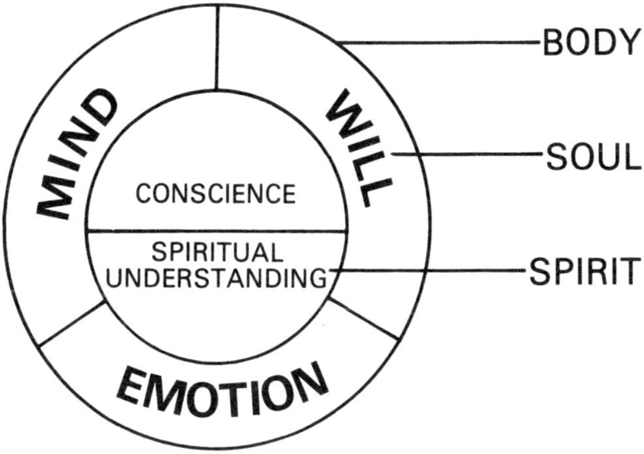

calls his "heart" (see Deuteronomy 4:29; Matthew 5:8). Man's intellect (mind), will and emotion comprise the soul which functions as his *self*-consciousness. The body, however, which houses both soul and spirit, is *world*-conscious by virtue of its senses.

It is through these senses (eyes, ears, touch, etc.), that God has ordained to reach our inner life (spirit/soul) through His Word. Thus, we preach and teach the truth, trusting the Holy Spirit to penetrate sin-benighted hearts.

Man has been likened to the Old Testament tabernacle which was structured in three parts: the outer court (body), the Holy place (soul), and the Holy of Holies (spirit).[8] Each section possessed its own light — the sun shone into the outer court, the candlestick illuminated the Holy place, and God's Shekinah glory filled the Holy of Holies. To think that these bodies can become God's dwelling place in Christ is beyond human comprehension! What a glorious privilege and potential God invested in Adam, only to be wrecked by sin. But thank God for redeeming grace in Christ by which man's potential is restored!

[8]Nee, *op. cit.*, 1:29.

Selected Passages for Meditation in Trying Circumstances

AGING

Job 12:12: "With the ancient is wisdom; and in length of days understanding."

Psalm 71:17-19: "O God, thou hast taught me from my youth: and hitherto have I declared thy wondrous works. Now also when I am old and grayheaded, O God, forsake me not; until I have shewed thy strength unto this generation, and thy power to every one that is to come."

See also Deuteronomy 34:7; Psalm 91:14-16; and Matthew 6:25-26.

ANGER AND HOSTILITY

Matthew 6:14-15: "For if ye forgive men their trespasses, your heavenly Father will also forgive you: But if ye forgive not men their trespasses, neither will your Father forgive your trespasses."

James 1:19-20: "Wherefore, my beloved brethren, let every man be swift to hear, slow to speak, slow to wrath: For the wrath of man worketh not the righteousness of God."

See also Proverbs 24:17-20; Luke 17:3-4; and Romans 13:8.

BEREAVEMENT

Psalm 42:11: "Why art thou cast down, O my soul? and why art thou disquieted within me: hope thou in God: for I shall yet praise him, who is the health of my countenance, and my God."

Matthew 5:4: "Blessed are they that mourn: for they shall be comforted."

See also Numbers 6:24-26; Job 5:8-11.

CONFUSION AND DOUBT

Isaiah 30:21: "And thine ears shall hear a word behind thee, saying, This is the way, walk ye in it, when ye turn to the right hand, and when ye turn to the left."

John 8:12: "Then spake Jesus again unto them, saying, I am the light of the world: he that followeth me shall not walk in darkness, but shall have the light of life."

See also Joshua 1:5; Jeremiah 29:11-13; and Romans 8:38-39.

CRISIS

Deuteronomy 31:8: "And the Lord, he it is that doth go before thee; he will be with thee, he will not fail thee, neither forsake thee: fear not, neither be dismayed."

Psalm 3:1-6: "Lord, how are they increased that trouble me! Many are they that rise up against me. Many there be which say of my soul, There is no help for him in God. Selah. But thou, O Lord, art a shield for me; my glory, and the lifter up of my head. I cried unto the Lord with my voice, and he heard me out of his holy hill. Selah. I laid me down and slept; I awaked; for the Lord sustained me. I will not be afraid of ten thousands of people, that have set themselves against me round about."

See also Psalm 34:6; Psalm 121:1-8; and Isaiah 41:10.

DEPRESSION

John 14:1: "Let not your heart be troubled; ye believe in God, believe also in me."

Romans 8:28-29: "And we know that all things work together for good to them that love God, to them who are the called according to his purpose. For whom he did foreknow, he also did predestinate to be conformed to the image of his Son, that he might be the firstborn among many brethren."

See also Job 22:29; Psalm 34:15-17; and Matthew 11:28-30.

DISAPPOINTMENT

Psalm 71:19-21: "Thy righteousness also, O God, is very high, who hast done great things: O God, who is like unto thee! Thou, which hast shewed me great and sore troubles, shalt quicken me again, and shalt bring me up again from the depths of the earth. Thou shalt increase my greatness, and comfort me on every side."

II Corinthians 4:17-18: "For our light affliction, which is but for a moment, worketh for us a far more exceeding and eternal weight of glory; While we look not at the things which are seen but at the things which are not seen: for the things which are seen are temporal; but the things which are not seen are eternal."

See also Psalm 130:1-6; Daniel 10:18-19; and Hebrews 12:11.

ENVY AND JEALOUSY

Proverbs 15:16-17: "Better is little with the fear of the Lord than great treasure and trouble therewith. Better is a dinner of herbs where love is, than a stalled ox and hatred therewith."

Galatians 5:25-26: "If we live in the Spirit, let us also walk in the Spirit. Let us not be desirous of vain glory, provoking one another, envying one another."

See also Psalm 37:34-36; I Corinthians 12:4-11; and James 3:13-18.

FAILURE

Psalm 57:1-3: "Be merciful unto me, O God, be merciful unto me: for my soul trusteth in thee: yea, in the shadow of thy wings will I make my refuge, until these calamities be overpast. I will cry unto God most high; unto God that performeth all things for me. He shall send from heaven, and save me from the reproach of him that would swallow me up. Selah. God shall send forth his mercy and his truth."

Habakkuk 3:19: "The Lord God is my strength, and he will make my fect like hinds' feet, and he will make me to walk upon mine high places."

See also I Samuel 16:7; Jeremiah 17:7-8; and Colossians 3:23.

FEAR

Psalm 27:1-3: "The Lord is my light and my salvation, whom shall I fear? The Lord is the strength of my life; of whom shall I be afraid? When the wicked, even mine enemies and my foes, came upon me to eat up my flesh, they stumbled and fell. Though a host should encamp against me, my heart shall not fear: though war should rise against me, in this will I be confident."

II Timothy 1:7: "For God hath not given us the spirit of fear; but of power, and of love, and of a sound mind."

See also Psalm 46:1-3; Psalm 56:3-4; and Isaiah 41:10-15.

HABITS (e.g., Drinking, Drugs, Smoking, etc.)

Psalm 40:1-3: "I waited patiently for the Lord; and he inclined unto me, and heard my cry. He brought me up also out of a horrible pit, out of the miry clay, and set my feet upon a rock, and established my goings. And he hath put a new song in my mouth, even praise unto our God: many shall see it, and fear, and shall trust in the Lord."

Philippians 4:13: "I can do all things through Christ which strengtheneth me."

See also Proverbs 20:1; Proverbs 23:29-35; Isaiah 59:1; II Corinthians 12:9; and Ephesians 5:17-20.

HOPELESSNESS

Psalm 23:1-6: "The Lord is my shepherd; I shall not want. He maketh me to lie down in green pastures: he leadeth me beside the still waters. He restoreth my soul: he leadeth me in the paths of righteousness for his name's sake. Yea, though I walk through the valley of the shadow of death, I will fear no evil: for thou art with me; thy rod and thy staff they comfort me. Thou preparest a table before me in the presence of mine enemies: thou anointest my head with oil; my cup runneth over. Surely goodness and mercy shall follow me all the days of my life: and I will dwell in the house of the Lord for ever."

Psalm 146:5: "Happy is he that hath the God of Jacob for his help, whose hope is in the Lord his God."

See also Psalm 71:5, 14; Isaiah 43:2; and I Peter 1:3.

HOSTILITY OR HATRED

Matthew 18:20-22: "For where two or three are gathered together in my name, there am I in the midst of them. Then came Peter to him, and said, Lord, how oft shall my brother sin against me, and I forgive him? till seven times? Jesus saith unto him, I say not unto thee, Until seven times: but, Until seventy times seven."

Luke 6:35-36: "But love ye your enemies, and do good, and lend, hoping for nothing again; and your reward shall be great, and ye shall be the children of the Highest: for he is kind unto the unthankful and to the evil. Be ye therefore merciful, as your Father also is merciful."

See also Matthew 5:43-45; Mark 11:25-26; and I John 4:7-12.

INSECURITY

John 6:37: "All that the Father giveth me shall come to me; and him that cometh to me I will in no wise cast out."

Hebrews 10:35-39: "Cast not away therefore your confidence, which hath great recompense of reward. For ye have need of patience, that, after ye have done the will of God, ye might receive the promise. For yet a little while, and he that shall come will come, and will not tarry. Now the just shall live by faith: but if any man draw back, my soul shall have no pleasure in him. But we are not of them who draw back unto perdition; but of them that believe to the saving of the soul."

See also Psalm 4:8; Psalm 37:25; Isaiah 50:7-9; and Hebrews 10:35-39.

LONELINESS

Psalm 142:4-6: "I looked on my right hand, and beheld, but there was no man that would know me: refuge failed me; no man cared for my soul. I cried unto thee, O Lord: I said, Thou art my refuge and my portion in the land of the living. Attend unto my cry; for I am brought very low: deliver me from my persecutors; for they are stronger than I."

John 14:18-20: "I will not leave you comfortless: I will come to you. Yet a little while, and the world seeth me no more; but ye see me: because I live, ye shall live also. At that day ye shall know that I am in my Father, and ye in me, and I in you."

See also John 16:32-33; Romans 14:8; and Revelation 3:20.

OPPRESSION

Deuteronomy 33:27: "The eternal God is thy refuge, and underneath are the everlasting arms: and he shall thrust out the enemy from before thee; and shall say, Destroy them."

Jeremiah 20:11: "But the Lord is with me as a mighty terrible one: therefore my persecutors shall stumble, and they shall not prevail: they shall be greatly ashamed; for they shall not prosper: their everlasting confusion shall never be forgotten."

See also Isaiah 51:11-13; Zephaniah 3:17-20; and Galatians 5:1.

REJECTION

Matthew 5:11: "Blessed are ye, when men shall revile you, and persecute you, and shall say all manner of evil against you falsely, for my sake."

II Timothy 2:1-3: "Thou therefore, my son, be strong in the grace that is in Christ Jesus. And the things that thou hast heard of me among many witnesses, the same commit thou to faithful men, who shall be able to teach others also. Thou therefore endure hardness, as a good soldier of Jesus Christ."

See also Luke 10:16; John 15:19-25; and II Corinthians 1:3-4.

REPENTANCE

Isaiah 55:7: "Let the wicked forsake his way, and the unrighteous man his thoughts: and let him return unto the Lord, and he will have mercy upon him; and to our God, for he will abundantly pardon."

Acts 3:19-21: "Repent ye therefore, and be converted, that your sins may be blotted out, when the times of refreshing shall come from the presence of the Lord; And he shall send Jesus Christ, which before was preached unto you: Whom the heaven must receive until the times of restitution of all things, which God hath spoken by the mouth of all his holy prophets since the world began."

See also Mark 2:16-17; Luke 15:7; and I John 1:8-9.

SICKNESS AND SUFFERING

Isaiah 40:28-31: "Hast thou not known? hast thou not heard, that the everlasting God, the Lord, the Creator of the ends of the earth, fainteth not, neither is weary? there is no searching of his understanding. He giveth power to the faint; and to them that have no might he increaseth strength. Even the youths shall faint and be weary, and the young men shall utterly fall: But they that wait upon the Lord shall renew their strength; they shall mount up with wings as eagles; they shall run, and not be weary; and they shall walk, and not faint."

Jeremiah 17:14: "Heal me, O Lord, and I shall be healed; save me, and I shall be saved: for thou art my praise."

See also Psalm 30:2-5; Proverbs 17:22; and Luke 4:40-41.

SIN AND GUILT

Psalm 51:1-4: "Have mercy upon me, O God, according to thy lovingkindness: according unto the multitude of thy tender mercies blot out my transgressions. Wash me throughly from mine iniquity, and cleanse me from my sin. For I acknowledge my transgressions: and my sin is ever before me. Against thee, thee only, have I sinned, and done this evil in thy sight: that thou mightest be justified when thou speakest, and be clear when thou judgest."

Isaiah 1:18: "Come now, and let us reason together, saith the Lord: though your sins be as scarlet, they shall be as white as snow; though they be red like crimson, they shall be as wool."

See also Isaiah 53:4-6; Isaiah 55:6-7; and Matthew 18:11.

SORROW

Psalm 61:1-4: "Hear my cry, O God; attend unto my prayer. From the end of the earth will I cry unto thee, when my heart is overwhelmed: lead me to the rock that is higher than I. For thou hast been a shelter for me, and a strong tower from the enemy. I will abide in thy tabernacle for ever: I will trust in the covert of thy wings. Selah."

James 5:10-11: "Take, my brethren, the prophets, who have spoken in the name of the Lord, for an example of suffering affliction, and of patience. Behold, we count them happy which endure. Ye have heard of the patience of Job, and have seen the end of the Lord; that the Lord is very pitiful, and of tender mercy."

See also Psalm 42:5; John 17:24-26; and I Peter 4:12-13.

TEMPTATION

I Corinthians 10:13: "There hath no temptation taken you but such as is common to man: but God is faithful, who will not suffer you to be tempted above that ye are able; but will with the temptation also make a way to escape, that ye may be able to bear it."

James 4:7: "Submit yourselves therefore to God. Resist the devil, and he will flee from you."

See also Psalm 62:5-7; Ephesians 6:11; and James 1:12-16.

TENSION

Romans 8:28-29: "And we know that all things work together for good to them that love God, to them who are the called according to his purpose. For whom he did foreknow, he also did predestinate to be conformed to the image of his Son, that he might be the firstborn among many brethren."

II Corinthians 4:8-9: "We are troubled on every side, yet not distressed; we are perplexed, but not in despair; Persecuted, but not forsaken; cast down, but not destroyed."

See also Proverbs 3:5-6; Philippians 4:6-7; and I Peter 5:7-9.

WORRY

Isaiah 26:3: "Thou wilt keep him in perfect peace, whose mind is stayed on thee: because he trusteth in thee."

Philippians 4:4-8: "Rejoice in the Lord alway: and again I say, Rejoice. Let your moderation be known unto all men.

The Lord is at hand. Be careful for nothing; but in every thing by prayer and supplication with thanksgiving let your requests be made known unto God. And the peace of God, which passeth all understanding, shall keep your hearts and minds through Christ Jesus. Finally, brethren, whatsoever things are true, whatsoever things are honest, whatsoever things are just, whatsoever things are pure, whatsoever things are lovely, whatsoever things are of good report; if there be any virtue, and if there be any praise, think on these things.''

See also Psalm 37:3-5; Matthew 6:24-33; and I Peter 5:7.

Bibliography

Adams, Jay E., *Competent to Counsel.* Nutley: Presbyterian and Reformed Publishing Company, 1970.

__________, *More Than Redemption.* Phillipsburg: Presbyterian and Reformed Publishing Company, 1979.

Bridges, Charles, *An Exposition of Proverbs.* Marshallton: The National Federation for Christian Education, 1846.

Brooks, Thomas, *Precious Remedies Against Satan's Devices With the Covenant of Grace.* London: Sovereign Grace Publishers, 1676.

Burton, Ernest DeWitt, *Spirit, Soul and Flesh.* Chicago: The University of Chicago Press, 1918.

Davis, Thomas K., *Mind and Spirit.* Boston: Sherman, French & Company, 1914.

Funk & Wagnalls, *Standard College Dictionary.* New York: Funk & Wagnalls Company, 1963.

Girdlestone, Robert Baker, *Synonyms of the Old Testament.* Grand Rapids: William B. Eerdmans Publishing Company, 1897.

Heard, J.B., *The Tripartite Nature of Man.* Edinburgh: T & T Clark, 1870.

Hill, David, *Greek Words and Hebrew Meanings.* Cambridge: Cambridge University Press, 1967.

Johnson, James E., *The Gift of a Sound Mind.* Scottdale: Herald Press, 1980.

Kautzsch, E., *Gesenius' Hebrew Grammar.* London: Oxford University Press, 1909.

Kiev, Ari, *The Courage to Live.* New York: Thomas Y. Crowell Publishers, 1979.

Klagsbrun, Francine, *Too Young to Die.* Boston: Houghton & Mifflin Company, 1976.

Lindsay, Hal, *Satan Is Alive and Well on Planet Earth.* Grand Rapids: Zondervan Publishing House, 1972.

Lloyd-Jones, Martyn D., *Spiritual Depression — Its Causes and Cure.* Grand Rapids: William B. Eerdmans Publishing Company, 1965.

McMillen, S.I., *None of These Diseases.* Westwood: Fleming H. Revell Company, 1963.

Murrell, Conrad, *Take Heed Brethren Lest. . . .* Zachary: Fires of Revival Publishers, n.d.

Nee, Watchman, *The Spiritual Man.* 3 vols. New York: Christian Fellowship Publishers, Inc., 1968.

Penn-Lewis, Jessie, *War on the Saints.* Nashville: The Lighthouse, n.d.

Rockstad, Ernest B., *The Healing of the Mind.* Andover: Faith and Life Publications, 1972.

Stewart, James A., *Heaven's Throne Gift.* Zachary: Milldale International Ministries, n.d.

Strauss, Richard L., *Win the Battle for Your Mind.* Wheaton: S.P. Publications, Inc., 1980.

Trench, Richard C., *Synonyms of the New Testament.* Grand Rapids: William B. Eerdmans Publishing Company, 1965.

Vanover, Terry, *A Medical Doctor Comments on Mental Illness.* Andover: Faith and Life Publications, n.d.

Vine, W.E., *An Expository Dictionary of New Testament Words.* 4 vols. Westwood: Fleming H. Revell Company, 1940.

Weaver, Edward E., *Mind and Health.* New York: The Macmillan Company, 1913.

Wilson, William. *Old Testament Word Studies.* McLcan: MacDonald Publishing Company, n.d.

Wright, Norman, *An Answer to Worry and Anxiety.* Irvine: Harvest House Publishers, 1976.

REVIVAL LITERATURE BOOKS PARTICULARLY RECOMMENDED BY DR. FINNIGAN

Heaven's Throne Gift

Open Windows

God's New Thing

The Lordship of Christ

The Invasion of Wales
by the Spirit

Still Waters

For a listing of other life-changing books, write to: